JourneyThrough®

1&2 Timothy

50 Daily Insights from God's Word **Robert M. Solomon**

Discovery House is affiliated
with Our Daily Bread Ministries.

Requests for permission to quote
from this book should be directed to:
Permissions Department
Discovery House
P.O. Box 3566
Grand Rapids, MI 49501
Or contact us by email at
permissionsdept@dhp.org

Design by Joshua Tan
Typeset by Grace Goh

ISBN 978-1-913135-09-6

Printed in the United Kingdom
First Printing in 2020

Foreword

Over the next 50 days, you will be reading and reflecting on 1 and 2 Timothy, two of the apostle Paul's last epistles. They deal with the ageing apostle's advice to Timothy, a younger pastor serving in Ephesus. They are personal in nature and yet have broad relevance to individual Christians and churches.

The central message in 1 Timothy is the importance of holding to the truth of the gospel of Jesus, which alone has the power to bring about human transformation. Belief produces behaviour; hence it is important to have the right beliefs in order to live a new life in Christ. "Watch your life and doctrine" (1 Timothy 4:16) summarises this well. In 2 Timothy, as Paul faces certain death, he encourages Timothy to be willing to suffer for the gospel. "I have fought the good fight, I have finished the race, I have kept the faith" (2 Timothy 4:7) provides a great testimony and model for every Christian.

I pray that over the next 50 days, you will let God speak to you through these ancient writings. May the timeless Word of God challenge you to assess your beliefs and behaviour, inspiring you to be faithful to Christ, right to the end.

Grace and Peace,
Robert M. Solomon

We're glad you've decided to join us on a journey into a deeper relationship with Jesus Christ!

For over 50 years, we have been known for our daily Bible reading notes, *Our Daily Bread*. Many readers enjoy the pithy, inspiring, and relevant articles that point them to God and the wisdom and promises of His unchanging Word.

Building on the foundation of *Our Daily Bread*, we have developed this devotional series to help believers spend time with God in His Word, book by book. We trust this daily meditation on God's Word will draw you into a closer relationship with Him through our Lord and Saviour, Jesus Christ.

How to use this resource

READ: This book is designed to be read alongside God's Word as you journey with Him. It offers explanatory notes to help you understand the Scriptures in fresh ways.

REFLECT: The questions are designed to help you respond to God and His Word, letting Him change you from the inside out.

RECORD: The space provided allows you to keep a diary of your journey as you record your thoughts and jot down your responses.

An Overview

Paul's two letters to Timothy were written near the end of his life, in AD 64 and AD 66/67. Both were deeply personal and dealt with pastoral issues. Timothy was by nature timid and, as one of Paul's successors, needed encouragement and strengthening. Paul urged him to remember his calling, keep faithful to Christ, and stay confident about the gospel. Timothy had to deal with false teachers in the church. He needed instructions on what and how to teach believers, and how to order life and ministry in the church in such a way that their conduct would convince the world of the gospel's truth and power to transform people. In order to fulfil his pastoral responsibilities, Timothy was urged to keep watch over his life and doctrine in the way Paul had demonstrated.

The structure of the book reflects these themes:

1 Timothy

1:1–2   Greetings

False Teachers Versus Faithful Teachers (1:3–20)

1:3–11   Warning against false teachers
1:12–20 Being a faithful teacher

How the Household of God Should Conduct Itself (2:1–6:21)

2:1–15   Worship in the church
3:1–16   Selecting church leaders
4:1–16   Dealing with false teaching
5:1–16   Helping widows
5:17–25 Respecting church elders
6:1–2   Slaves and masters
6:3–10   Warning for the rich
6:11–19 An exhortation for the pastor
6:20–21 Closing remarks and benediction

2 Timothy

United with Christ (1:1–18)

1:1–2   Knowing identity and calling
1:3–7   Knowing Christian heritage
1:8–18   United with Christ in service and suffering

Useful to Christ (2:1–26)

2:1–13   The right attitude to ministry
2:14–19 The meditation and application of Scripture
2:20–26 Ministering to the lost

Unlike the World (3:1–4:5)

3:1–9   The terrible world and its people
3:10–17 Christian character in a terrible world
4:1–5   Christian ministry in a terrible world

Faithful to the End (4:6–22)

4:6–8   Preparing for the end
4:9–15   Personal needs at the end
4:16–22 Faithful to the end

Day 1

Read 1 Timothy 1:1–2

n all of his 13 epistles in the New Testament, Paul begins with a salutation—a standard practice in his day. The writer and recipient are identified and a greeting is added.

In three of Paul's epistles, the salutation has noticeable differences. These are called the Pastoral Epistles—1 and 2 Timothy, and Titus. They are addressed to specific individuals and use warm terms of endearment: "my true son in the faith" (1 Timothy 1:2); "my dear son" (2 Timothy 1:2); "my true son in our common faith" (Titus 1:4). Except for Philemon, all the other Pauline epistles are addressed more generally to churches.

This more personal and intimate nature of the Pastoral Epistles is further distinguished by the greeting used in two of them. While all of Paul's epistles mention "grace" and "peace" in the salutation, the epistles to Timothy add the word "mercy".

Jews were used to greeting one another with "shalom" (peace). It was therefore unsurprising that Jesus greeted His disciples by saying, "Peace be with you" (John 20:19, 26). Christian practice continued this tradition. It also added the word "grace", which became an important concept in Christian doctrine (Romans 3:23–24; Ephesians 2:8). It therefore became common to have the words "grace and peace" in Christian greetings, as we see in Paul's epistles.

In 1 and 2 Timothy, Paul adds "mercy" in the salutation because he is mindful of the abundance of God's mercy (Ephesians 2:4) that was extended to him. He is deeply aware that God had forgiven him. Twice he testifies, "I was shown mercy" (1 Timothy 1:13,16).

Mercy means not receiving what you deserve, while grace means receiving what you don't deserve.

In forgiving us for our treachery against Him, receiving us as His prodigal children, and showering us with His love, God shows us both mercy and grace. The result is the all-rounded peace (within and in all relationships) that the word "shalom" conveys. We must think deeply about God's amazing grace and mercy, and drink constantly from them. Then the peace of God will replace our restlessness.

ThinkThrough

Reflect on the reality of God's grace, mercy, and peace in your life (suggestion: do it with the cross of Jesus in mind). How can you thank God for these gifts and grow deeply in them?

What opportunities do you have to share with others what God's grace, mercy, and peace mean to you?

Day 2

Read 1 Timothy 1:3–7

Paul had left Timothy behind in Ephesus to provide leadership in the church as his representative (1 Timothy 1:3). There were things to be sorted out. One of the emerging problems was the presence of dubious teachers in the church. These men, for various reasons, had "departed" from the faith (v. 6). They had become proud and thought too highly of themselves. They were in fact ignorant teachers who "[did] not know what they [were] talking about" (v. 7).

These teachers were not just dubious but also downright dangerous. They were spreading false doctrines and misleading Christians. In focusing on such unhelpful subjects as myths (perhaps Jewish and pagan fables) and "endless genealogies" (perhaps laborious or mystical Jewish genealogies), they were bringing about much confusion and controversy in the church (vv. 3–4). The gospel of Jesus was being forgotten as such false teachers led people away from the true path of Christian discipleship into dead ends.

One way to test whether a teaching is in line with God's truth is to examine its outcome. Belief determines behaviour, and that is why Paul insists that those who taught false doctrines must be challenged and rebuked. Believing God's truth leads to true godliness. Here, (v. 5) it is characterised by a "pure heart" (holiness of life), a "good conscience" (clean motives), and a "sincere faith" (lack of hypocrisy). Contrast this with the ill effects of false doctrine: "controversial speculations" (v. 4), "meaningless talk" (v. 6), and apostasy (v. 6).

Faithful teachers of the Word aim to bring about divine love in their hearers (v. 5). Their ministry is aligned to God's work, not against it. False teachers, on the other hand, do not produce godliness in their lives or ministry. We can identify false teachers and false teaching by examining them in the light of Scripture, and by assessing their content, motives, and results.

We should also examine our own lives—whether the teachings and doctrines that we are feeding on are producing true godliness in us. This is a necessary task in the Internet age, where almost anything and everything can be seen on websites and in chain emails.

Can you identify some modern versions of "myths" and "genealogies" in the church? Why are they harmful?

How do you think a pure heart, good conscience, and sincere faith are connected with the manifestation of divine love in a person?

Day 3

Read 1 Timothy 1:8–11

We are not sure what the false teachers were teaching in Ephesus, but from what Paul writes, we can guess that it could have had something to do with Old Testament law. They promoted themselves as teachers of the law (1 Timothy 1:7). Perhaps they were distorting the gospel ("sound doctrine", v. 10) by teaching a legalistic Christian faith—that we are saved by practising religious piety. In that case, theirs would have been a religion of the flesh, a salvation that is rooted in self-effort, resulting in self-glorification.

In every age of church history, such brands of legalistic Christianity have emerged to turn people away from the "gospel concerning the glory" of Christ (v. 11). How do we avoid getting into such doctrinal deviations? One way is to do away with the law altogether and ignore it. We then end up with a "grace is good, law is bad" kind of thinking. We can take up the Reformation cry—grace alone—and reject any role for the law in Christian living. But that is not how the great Reformer John Calvin saw it.

Calvin pointed out three purposes of the law, according to the Bible. Firstly, it is a mirror that shows the character of God as well as our own sinfulness. Secondly, it acts to restrain evil among people—imagine how anarchy would break out if there is no sense of divine law. Thirdly, it shows us what pleases God and guides us in our behaviour.

We find all three purposes in this passage. The law is made "for lawbreakers and rebels" (v. 9). Paul mentions some of the Ten Commandments in the passage (vv. 9–10). He also mentions "slave traders" (compare this with human trafficking) and homosexuals. Lawbreakers are exposed by the law and also restrained to some extent.

But we also note that "the law is good if one uses it properly" (v. 8). The law is a guide for Christian behaviour. We are not saved by keeping the law; instead, God saves us and enables us with His Spirit to keep His moral law, which reflects His character and how He has made us. When used in this way, the law is good.

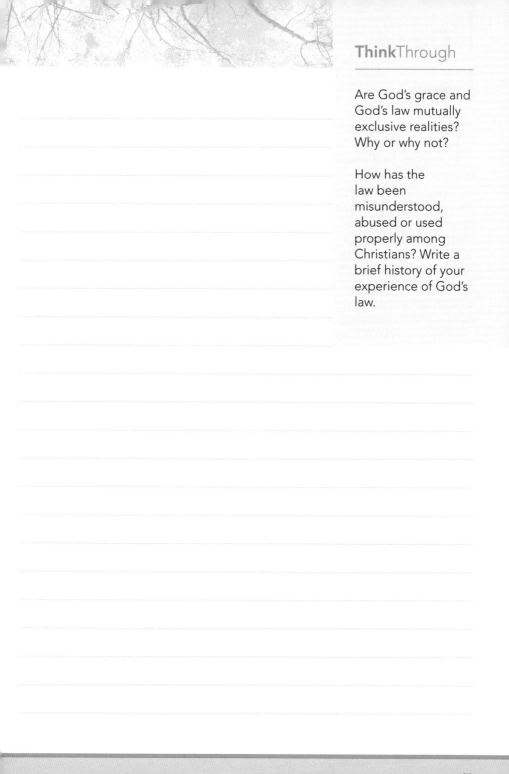

ThinkThrough

Are God's grace and God's law mutually exclusive realities? Why or why not?

How has the law been misunderstood, abused or used properly among Christians? Write a brief history of your experience of God's law.

Day 4

Read 1 Timothy 1:12–17

The sound doctrine of the gospel of Christ produces wonderfully transformed lives. Paul himself was a marvellous example.

He confesses that at one time, before he knew Jesus, he was "a blasphemer and a persecutor and a violent man" (1 Timothy 1:13). As a self-righteous Pharisee (Philippians 3:5) proud of his religious credentials and zeal, he thought he was serving God. But he suffered from the twin conditions of ignorance (he did not recognise Jesus for who He is) and unbelief (he did not take seriously whatever little information he had about Jesus). As a result, he became a violent persecutor of Christians.

But God showered His grace and mercy on Paul (1 Timothy 1:13,14,16), converted him and, remarkably, made him into a key apostle. God's gracious choices are full of mystery because they often involve the most unlikely of people. Why did God choose you and me to be His children?

It is possible that as we progress in our Christian lives, we may forget how merciful God has been to us. We may begin believing that God is fortunate to have us in His kingdom! In Paul's case, the older he grew, the more he realised his sinful condition and his dire need for God's forgiveness and mercy. Therefore, although he had argued in one of his earliest epistles (written in AD 49) that he was as good an apostle as any other (Galatians 1:1, 2:11), six years later he described himself as "the least of the apostles" who did "not even deserve to be called an apostle" (1 Corinthians 15:9). After another five years had passed, he considered himself "less than the least of all the Lord's people" (Ephesians 3:8). Finally, in 1 Timothy (four years later), Paul referred to himself as "the worst of sinners"—not once but twice (1 Timothy 1:15–16).

Paul became increasingly humble as his knowledge of God grew— a sure sign that he was drawing closer to God. Notice Paul's description of the majesty and glory of God (1 Timothy 1:17) and the "immense patience" of Christ (v. 16). As a recipient of God's transforming grace and mercy, Paul is convinced that Jesus is the Saviour of sinners (v. 15). Hence he was totally committed to preaching the gospel (v. 12).

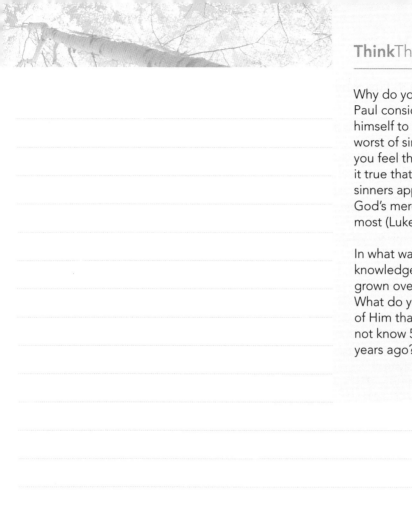

Why do you think Paul considered himself to be the worst of sinners? Do you feel the same? Is it true that the worst sinners appreciate God's mercy the most (Luke 7:47)?

In what way has your knowledge of God grown over time? What do you know of Him that you did not know 5 or 10 years ago?

Day 5

Read 1 Timothy 1:18–20

This epistle begins and ends with Paul's charge to Timothy. Paul begins by urging Timothy to correct the false teachings and to deal effectively with those who were spreading such dangerous doctrines in the church. He concludes by instructing his spiritual son to watch his own life and doctrine (1 Timothy 4:16).

Timothy was ordained or commissioned by the laying on of hands by the body of elders (4:14), which included Paul (2 Timothy 1:6). At this time, a prophecy was uttered that probably had to do with Timothy's future ministry, and a "gift of God" was given to Timothy. It is clear that God was very much behind Timothy's call to ministry. He had equipped Timothy for the task. Paul therefore urges Timothy to be mindful of these truths and to live accordingly.

By pursuing God's call and living it out, Timothy would be able to "fight the battle well, holding on to faith and a good conscience" (1 Timothy 1:18–19). One of Paul's favourite metaphors for Christian discipleship and ministry is the "fight". This refers to athletic wrestling in the Greek Games and to the reality of struggle and the necessity for resilience and discipline in the Christian life. Many choose the easier life of compromise and spiritual unfaithfulness. They may end up surviving or even thriving in the ungodly world, but losing their souls (Mark 8:36). Timothy is urged to hold on to the faith and a good conscience (1 Timothy 1:5), and to never let go.

It is important to choose the right way rather than the easy way—even when we are persecuted and life becomes difficult. We should not be like Hymenaeus (1:20; 2 Timothy 2:17) and Alexander, who "suffered shipwreck with regard to the faith" (1:19–20). They were possibly the leading false teachers who had gone astray, and were probably excommunicated as a result.

Verse 20 mentions that they were "handed over to Satan" to learn not to blaspheme (which indicates the falsehood they taught about God). They were not totally abandoned to destruction, but the church needed to be protected from them, leaving its doors open for them when they had repented.

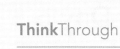

ThinkThrough

How can Christians shipwreck their faith? What steps must you take to hold firmly to the faith in order to fight the good fight?

The false teachers were handed over to Satan. Imagine what would have happened to them. How does being part of the church confer spiritual protection?

Day 6

Read 1 Timothy 2:1–7

Mahatma Gandhi told Dr E. Stanley Jones, a missionary to India, that he had no problem with the Christ of Christianity; his problem was with Christians. He observed that many of them did not live according to the teachings of Christ.

There are many people like Gandhi who are turned away from Christ because of the bad testimony of Christians. **It is important to remember that Christians are, to the watching world, the living examples of the truth and power of the gospel.**

Ideal Christian witness (that attracts rather than repels) is marked by "peaceful and quiet lives in all godliness and holiness" (1 Timothy 2:2). Such living is good and pleasing to God (v. 3), for it reflects the character of God and leads to the salvation of people.

Paul portrays God as wanting "all people to be saved" (v. 4, see 2 Peter 3:9). And there is only one Saviour for all, the Lord Jesus Christ who "gave himself as a ransom for all people" (v. 6). Jesus paid the price upon the cross to redeem all people from their sins by offering himself as the ransom. He is the only Mediator between sinful men and the one holy God (for there are no other gods) and, therefore, the only One who can bring salvation to all (v. 5).

The point is that because Jesus is the only Saviour for all, we should not distract or divert people away from Jesus—that would be an awful thing. We should not become obstacles to the salvation of others because of our unfaithfulness or disobedience.

The faithful teaching of sound doctrine brings about truly beautiful and godly lives, which in turn help to bring others to Christ by convincing them of the truth of the gospel (1 Peter 2:12). Paul was totally committed to his ministry as a herald (preacher), apostle (leader), and teacher of this true faith (1 Timothy 2:7) that saves and transforms people.

It is therefore important to pray for all (so that all can be saved), including world leaders who need to rule responsibly so that the social environment is conducive to godliness and evangelism.

ThinkThrough

Make as many connections as you can between holiness and the evangelisation of the world. What are common reasons why people are turned off by the church?

How would you explain that Jesus is the only Saviour of the whole human race? What are the implications of this for your witness and prayer life?

Read 1 Timothy 2:8–15

Paul continues to discuss Christian behaviour that will help to convince people outside the church of the truth and power of the gospel. Here the focus is on what goes on in the church—in particular how the church worships God. Paul had already dealt with problems in the Corinthian church, where rowdy and disorderly worship turned unbelievers away (1 Corinthians 14:22–25). In Ephesus the problems seem to be disunity, and the lack of modesty and submission.

Imagine a church where the men pray fervently, but also fight with one another fiercely. No one would be convinced of the gospel from their behaviour. Therefore Paul requires that men in church pray without "anger or disputing" (1 Timothy 2:8). It does not mean that there should be no differences of opinion at all in church, but differences should be handled in a mature Christian way that shows a deeper unity in Christ. It is for this reason that Jesus prayed for the unity of His followers, so that the world might believe in Him (John 17:21,23).

In sophisticated Ephesus, the immodesty of fashionable society was being imported by some women into the church. Therefore Paul has to insist that Christian women "dress modestly, with decency and propriety" (1 Timothy 2:9). Rather than focus on their hairstyles, jewellery, and expensive and stylish clothes, they should spend time and energy on their inner character and good deeds (2:10). **Character is far more important than cosmetics.** After all, what adorns the doctrine of God is not our dressing or cosmetic attractiveness, but our inner character and outward good deeds (Titus 2:9–10).

There was also the problem of unsubmissive women, who in their newfound Christian freedom were doing things in church that destroyed their witness in a society where such things were looked upon negatively. It is in this context that Paul forbids women to teach men or exercise authority over them in church (1 Timothy 2:11–12).

Modern ears may find this offensive or irrelevant, although Paul uses biblical principles drawn from creation and the fall to argue his case. Paul seems to suggest that motherhood may be an important aspect of a woman's calling (2:15). Other biblical passages will give us a fuller picture of the place of women in the home, church, and society (Genesis 1:27, 2:18; Judges 4:4–5; Proverbs 31:10–31; Luke 8:1–3; Acts 21:9; Romans 16:1–6; 1 Corinthians 11:3,8–9, 14:34–35,40; Galatians 3:28; Ephesians 5:22–24; Colossians 3:18; 1 Timothy 5:14; Titus 2:3–5; 1 Peter 3:1,4–6).

What modern versions of disunity, immodesty, and insubordination do you find in the church? How do they drive people away from Jesus?

Can you remember Bible passages that speak of the dignity and ministry of women (e.g. Galatians 3:28; Acts 16:1; John 20:17–18)? How would you reconcile these verses with what Paul instructs in this passage?

Day 8

Read 1 Timothy 3:1–7

More people could be convinced of the gospel's truth if the behaviour of Christians corresponded with their beliefs. Beginning with his own experience of God's transforming grace in Christ, Paul goes on to show how worship and behaviour in the church has an impact on those outside the church. He then moves on in this passage to deal with the kind of leaders we should have in church, and their desired character and behaviour.

Paul lists the qualifications of an *episkopos* (translated as bishop or overseer). Many scholars consider this leadership position to be similar to that of an elder (Titus 1:5–6). An overseer has a noble task (1 Timothy 3:1) and must be "above reproach" (v. 2), that is, he must not have serious character flaws. Paul's list focuses on the character of the overseer rather than his task (which would involve watching over the flock, protecting, nurturing, guiding, and leading them). The most critical task is shown in the words "able to teach" (v. 2), which is connected with the unique role of overseers (1 Timothy 5:17).

The rest of Paul's list spells out how the overseer must be a mature (1 Timothy 3:6) and godly Christian. He must not be guilty of sinful passions or habits—no drunkenness, violence, quarrelsome attitude or greed (3:3). Instead, he should reflect Christ-likeness—temperate, self-controlled, hospitable, and gentle (vv. 2–3). He must have "a good reputation with outsiders" (v. 7) so that his life and ministry do not become a stumbling block to believers and those outside the church. He must live in such a way, including living an exemplary family life, with marital faithfulness ("faithful to his wife", v. 2; literally a "one-woman man") and domestic stability (v. 4). He will gain the respect of all ("respectable", v. 2) as he lives out what we read in Isaiah 32:8, "the noble man makes noble plans, and by noble deeds they stands".

The church must choose leaders after God's own heart—those who are godly and serious about their leadership role and ministry, and who will inspire people and bring them closer to God (Jeremiah 3:15).

ThinkThrough

Why do you think
Paul focused on
character more than
skills? Can the ways
in which the church
chooses its leaders
and ministers be
improved?

In what ways can
a leader become
proud, fall into
disgrace, or be
entrapped by the
devil (1 Timothy
3:6–7)? If you are
a leader, how can
you guard yourself?
If not, how can
you pray for your
leaders?

Read 1 Timothy 3:8–13

The ministry of deacons in the church supports and complements that of elders. In Paul's list of qualifications for deacons, the focus is again on character rather than tasks. The significant difference between the two lists is the ability to teach. For elders (or overseers), teaching is their prime responsibility.

This does not mean that deacons have nothing to do with God's Word. They are expected to "keep hold of the deep truths of the faith" (1 Timothy 3:9). They must have a good knowledge of Scripture and be committed to its teachings. We must always remember that belief is connected with behaviour; knowledge of Scripture is important for the development of Christian character.

Like the overseer, the deacon's life must win the respect of others (3:8). There must not be evidence of drunkenness, greed, or lack of integrity ("dishonest gain") in his life. He must also be a one-woman man and manage his family well (3:12).

Many interpreters consider verse 11 as referring to deaconesses rather than the wives of deacons (literally "the women" in Greek). If so, Paul also requires women holding the office of a deaconess (Romans 16:1) to be respectable people. They should not talk ill of others and should gain the trust of others through their sober living.

It is easy to think that those who are in "lesser" positions in church are excused from the high standards of Christian character and behaviour. But this is not true. Note the "same way" in 1 Timothy 3:8 and how Paul expects the same high standards of personal integrity and godliness in deacons as in elders. It is instructive that when the early church selected the first seven deacons, the qualification was that the men should be "full of the Spirit and wisdom" (Acts 6:3).

Whatever our position or role in the church is, as members of the body of Christ, tasked and gifted for various ministries, we must show the highest standards of personal integrity, seriousness, and Christ-like character. This will not be possible without a good knowledge of the Word of God and the fullness of the Holy Spirit.

How can the church "test" people (1 Timothy 3:10) to see whether they are qualified for various ministries and positions in the church?

Paul refers to those "who have served well" (3:13). What do they gain?

Day 10

Read 1 Timothy 3:14–16

Bad teaching is connected with bad behaviour while good teaching (sound doctrine) produces true transformation and godliness. Paul has shown how our worship, community life, leadership, and ministry should testify to the truth and power of the gospel. The phrase, "how people ought to conduct themselves in God's household" (1 Timothy 3:15), reveals what was in Paul's mind.

The church should be a living demonstration of the gospel. If it fails in this, its mission will be seriously affected. It must realise its noble role to be the "pillar and foundation of the truth" (3:15). It supports and displays the truth.

Additionally, the conduct of the church and its members should convince people that it is "the church of the living God" (3:15). We are reminded of Zechariah's prophecy, "In those days ten people from all languages and nations will take firm hold of one Jew by the hem of his robe and say, 'Let us go with you, because we have heard that God is with you' " (Zechariah 8:23).

All these things are possible because of the "mystery from which true godliness springs" (1 Timothy 3:16), which is all to do with Jesus.

The word "mystery" in the Bible refers to truth that has not been known, but is now revealed. This mystery is about Jesus, who appeared 2,000 years ago. His life is traced in what appears to be a hymn or creedal statement. Jesus "appeared in the body" (referring to the incarnation and refuting heresies that denied His humanity). He was "vindicated by the Spirit" (through His resurrection, therefore showing His deity). He was "seen by angels" (demonstrating His victory in heaven and on earth). He was "preached among the nations" and was believed by many. We are all the result of this preaching mission. And He "was taken up in glory". This may refer to the ascension, but because it appears as the last statement, it could also refer to the second coming of Christ in glory.

Jesus is the mystery and glory of the church. Our tiny stories have meaning because of His story, which must be demonstrated by the church.

ThinkThrough

Is there any way in which the church has failed to convince others that it really belongs to the living God? How does the church guard the truth of the gospel?

Why do you think Paul used the phrase, "the mystery of godliness"? Consider Colossians 1:25–27. How does the story of Jesus transform your old story into a new one?

Day 11

Read 1 Timothy 4:1–5

False and harmful teaching is unable to produce Christ-like character and behaviour. It is also dangerous because of the spiritual realities behind it.

False teachers are the human agents through whom such heresy is spread. They are "hypocritical liars" (1 Timothy 4:2), and do not teach the truth nor practise it; their consciences have been "seared". This is the fourth time Paul mentions the conscience (see 1 Timothy 1:5,19; 3:9). The conscience is a moral compass that warns us if we break God's law, but it can be weakened (1 Corinthians 8:10) by wrong social "programming" and seared by repeated disobedience. It needs to be educated by the Word and the Spirit (Psalm 119:11; John 16:8–11, 17:17; Hebrews 9:13–14, 10:16,22).

A seared conscience has lost its sensitivity (like the way the tongue feels numb after being scalded by boiling soup). It will not "sound the alarm" when its owner dabbles in evil. Paul highlights the spiritual forces of deceiving spirits (demons) at work when someone peddles heresy (1 Timothy 4:1). Satan, who specialises in blinding the minds of unbelievers (2 Corinthians 4:4), deploys his minions to deceive and deaden the consciences of false teachers so that they can do much damage in the church. Paul is aware of this and is deeply concerned about it. The Holy Spirit himself had revealed to Paul that in "later times" (or "last days", referring to the era from Pentecost to Christ's second coming; 2 Timothy 3:1; Hebrews 1:2), such deception would take place, making some "abandon the faith" (1 Timothy 4:1) and become apostate (renouncing the faith).

The false teachers taught a misguided asceticism (harsh self-discipline) that denied the creation. "God saw all that he had made, and it was very good" (Genesis 1:31). This included the creation of a man and a woman, the institution of marriage, and sex within marriage. The false teachers were forbidding people from marrying (a Gnostic idea) and eating certain foods (a Judaistic idea). The heresies in the early church had such roots that threatened the purity of the gospel, and the joy and well-being of Christians.

All good gifts created and instituted by God can be received with prayerful thanksgiving, remembering they were consecrated by God's Word, for He declared what He had created to be good.

Satan tempts people to eat the "forbidden fruit" (Genesis 3:1–7) or makes them refuse what God has given. How does he do it? What evidence of both deceptions do you find today?

In what ways can the conscience malfunction? How do you think it is educated by the Word and the Spirit? What is the state of your conscience?

Day 12

Read 1 Timothy 4:6–10

Timothy has a hugely important task at hand. In view of the serious damage that false teachers can do, and in view of the need to ensure that God's people conduct themselves well in God's household, it is of utmost importance that he serves as a "good minister of Christ Jesus" (1 Timothy 4:6).

A good minister holds firmly to God's truth. Paul reminds Timothy of being "nourished on the truths of the faith" and the "good teaching" that he had sincerely followed (v. 6). It is easier to abandon the truth by pursuing untrue "godless myths" and superstitious "old wives' tales" (v. 7). These things were very popular and were making the false teachers famous. As a good pastor, Timothy must teach what is true and central to the gospel of Jesus, and not be distracted by what may be popular or peripheral.

The truth is the gospel—it's about the "Saviour of all people", our need to believe in Him, and our need to "put our hope in the living God" (v. 10). Holding on to the gospel will result in the completion of God's mission and the salvation of people. Abandoning it for heresies and myths will have disastrous consequences.

Timothy must not only guard his doctrine (which has practical results), but he must also guard his life. Paul urges him, "train yourself to be godly" (v. 7). How do we do this? It suggests that just as an athlete must be disciplined and determined to remain fit and grow in strength, so too must Christ's disciple in spiritual matters.

There are certain spiritual disciplines that are essential for spiritual fitness and growth. These include Bible reading and meditation, prayer, and worship. Obeying God constantly is required. The diligent fulfilment of Christian duties and wholehearted service for God are ways in which disciples train themselves to be godly. Such training will have wonderful spiritual results in your life and ministry.

Lazy Christians do not become godly. Those who neglect their spiritual disciplines and regular times of communion with the Lord will not grow in godliness or usefulness to the Lord.

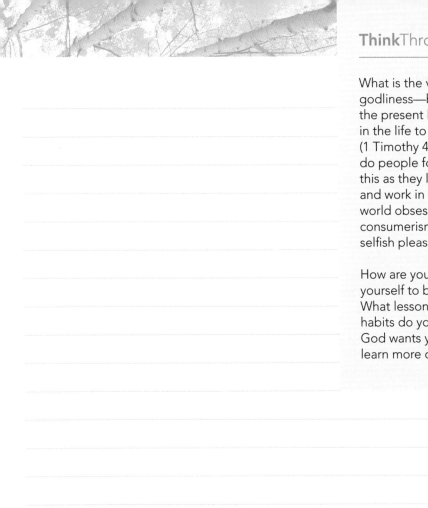

What is the value of godliness—both in the present life and in the life to come (1 Timothy 4:8)? Why do people forget this as they live and work in a busy world obsessed with consumerism and selfish pleasure?

How are you training yourself to be godly? What lessons and habits do you think God wants you to learn more deeply?

Day 13

Read 1 Timothy 4:11–16

Timothy was a young pastor. Scholars differ in their estimation of his age. Some put it as between late 20s and mid-30s, while others believe it was between mid-30s and 40s. Regardless, it is not easy for a young pastor to instruct and teach older people. In Asian societies, older people may tell a younger person, "The salt I have eaten is more than the rice you have eaten!" This is like saying, "Young man, I know life better than you do."

Perhaps anticipating similar challenges for Timothy, Paul fortifies him by saying, "Don't let anyone look down on you because you are young" (1 Timothy 4:12). Timothy has to exercise the authority given to him by God and affirmed by the body of elders at his ordination (v. 14). This authority is not his own, but one derived from his calling. There is no better way to exercise it than by being exemplary in his discipleship. Therefore Timothy is to exemplify godliness in what he believes and in how he lives—in his character, conversations, and relationships (v. 12).

Timothy must not only set a godly example, but also continue to exhort his flock faithfully. This is best done by preaching, teaching, and the public reading of Scripture (v. 13). This is the ministry to which Timothy was called, having been appropriately and adequately equipped by God (v. 14).

Paul summarises both points (example and exhortation) by reiterating, "Watch your life and doctrine closely" (v. 16). Watch who you are becoming. Watch what you are doing. What sort of example are you setting? How are you feeding your flock? Are you a good minister in your inward character and your outward ministry? Such diligent discipleship and ministry (v. 15) will result in the salvation of both the pastor and the flock (v. 16)—in terms of their sanctification and growth in holiness (v. 15).

The word "watch" indicates careful attention that should be paid to life and doctrine.

It is like the way many people monitor their health with eagle eyes, taking quick and appropriate action whenever they notice threats or deterioration. How is it that people who give so much attention to their physical health so carelessly neglect their spiritual health?

What sort of example are you to your family members, friends, colleagues, and others? Is God saying something to you about specific areas that need attention?

Timothy is urged to give himself wholly to his calling and to make good progress in his discipleship (1 Timothy 4:15). What steps do you need to take to answer this same challenge?

Day 14

Read 1 Timothy 5:1–2

Gregory the Great wrote a classic in the sixth century that is still used for pastoral training today. In his *Pastoral Rule*, he outlines 34 types of people in the church and how a pastor must minister to them in different ways. One shoe size will not fit all feet.

There are different categories of people in church—old and young, men and women, well-educated and illiterate, rich and poor, married and single or divorced or widowed. In many places, there are also different ethnic and language groups. Ministry to each and everyone in the church must therefore be done with great care and sensitivity.

Whatever the differences may be, there are some basic principles and values that must be observed in all relationships in church. Paul spells them out, illustrating them with some of the different categories of church members.

Firstly, respect. How should Timothy instruct older men? Age is not a barrier to the ministry of the Word. When older men are wrong, they need to be rebuked, but not in a harsh tone. When they are faltering, they need to be exhorted. In doing all these, Timothy must show respect (Leviticus 19:32; 1 Peter 2:17), the kind a son shows his father (1 Timothy 5:1). Scripture commands us to honour our parents (Exodus 20:12).

Secondly, love. Timothy is to love younger men as brothers (1 Timothy 5:1). He should not bully or abuse them.

Third, purity. Timothy is to consider all women (5:2) as either mothers (older women) or sisters (younger women). This is necessary if his life is to have "absolute purity".

These three attitudes are necessary in all our relationships. They represent the godliness that arises from a Christ-like character. They prevent one from becoming arrogant, indifferent, or lustful.

We must also notice how Paul describes the various relationships in terms of family relationships: fathers, mothers, brothers, and sisters. We are challenged to think of the church as a family and to treat fellow believers as our own family members. This is how we ought to conduct ourselves in "God's household" (1 Timothy 3:15). Then, others will believe that the gospel is true and able to completely change people and communities.

Paul moves from "honour" (1 Timothy 5:3 ESV) to "double honour" (5:17) to "all honour" (6:1 ESV). How can respect and honour be given to fellow believers?

The opposite of love is indifference. How can Christians truly love one another with absolute purity? Why is thinking of others as family members helpful?

Day 15

Read 1 Timothy 5:3–16

The church in Ephesus had widows in its community. From its earliest days, the church exercised its responsibility to take care of widows (Acts 6:1). This was in line with scriptural teaching as well as practical necessity.

God expects His people to help the needy, such as widows and orphans (Deuteronomy 24:17–21, 26:12–13, 27:19; Isaiah 1:17; James 1:27). In ancient societies, widows and orphans were unable to support themselves through employment. If left unsupported, they could end up as slaves, prostitutes, or beggars, neglected or abused by society.

The early church had to work out a practical way of assisting widows. Paul deals with some helpful principles here.

Firstly, a proper attitude is required towards widows. Unlike sinful and selfish society, which tends to neglect or put down widows, Christians must give "proper recognition to those widows who are really in need" (1 Timothy 5:3). In the English Standard Version, this phrase is translated as "honour widows". In other words, we are to honour them in the same way older people, elders, and masters are to be honoured.

Secondly, not all widows need to be supported by the church. Those with families should be taken care of by them (v. 4). It honours and pleases God when Christians take care of their needy relatives. It is best for younger widows to be remarried so that they can do good by bringing up children and managing their families (v. 14). This will save them from idling away their lives fruitlessly (v. 13) or being the subject of slander (v. 14). They will also relieve the church of the burden of having to support them (v. 16), so that it can focus on the really needy widows.

There are, therefore, certain criteria for putting widows on the list to be helped by the church. One is that they must have no family members and no option of remarriage ("over sixty", v. 9). Another is that they must be godly women who had been faithful to their husbands and who are recognised for their good deeds— both at home, in the church, and in larger society (v. 10).

These are practical principles that the church can apply today in caring for the needy. The church, as Paul paints it, should be an orderly and caring one—a great witness for the Lord.

What needy groups are there in your church? How is the church helping them? Is the help that is given orderly and adequate?

Why is there a need to honour those who are often neglected or ignored by society? How can Christians do this better?

Day 16

Read 1 Timothy 5:17–20

Paul now turns his attention to how the church should treat its ministry leadership. He refers to the elders in the church and points to their essential duties: directing the affairs of the church, as well as preaching and teaching (1 Timothy 5:17). There are two things the believers must give them: respect and financial support.

Firstly, elders who are called to minister in the church as shepherds (Acts 20:28) are to be given "double honour" (1 Timothy 5:17). In other words, they are to be highly respected.

This is particularly relevant in our present day, when respect for those in authority is rapidly disappearing. A modern sense of equality, a highly individualistic perspective (the authority of the self is seen as greater), and a suspicious and critical attitude towards leadership further erode the authority of leaders. Of course, in some cases, the poor example of pastors and leaders does not help promote respect, especially when they are caught in sin or if they abuse their position.

Pastors and elders are officers instituted by God.
They carry an authority derived from their divine calling and the authority delegated to them by the church. It is not an authority that is inherent in them, but one that is given to them by nature of their ministerial office. This authority must be respected if the church is not to become dysfunctional and chaotic.

This does not mean, however, that elders have absolute authority. If they sin, they can be taken to task through a public rebuke (1 Timothy 5:20). The church must handle complaints against them carefully (5:19). But a basic respect is due to elders and pastors.

Secondly, pastors and elders who devote their time solely to the ministry should be adequately supported for their earthly needs.

Remember the saying, "as poor as a church mouse"? The attitude that pastors and full-time Christian workers should suffer on the edge of poverty must be resisted. Paul quotes Scripture (5:18)—"Do not muzzle an ox while it is treading out the grain" (Deuteronomy 25:4) and "The worker deserves his wages" (Luke 10:7, quoting Christ)—to support his point that pastors must be adequately supported.

How do pastors exercise their authority properly or abuse it? How can church members give their pastors "double honour"? Is there something you can do to honour your pastor?

How can the church ensure that the "worker" and his "wages" are related justly and proportionately? Do you think the pastors and Christian workers you know are adequately supported? Why is this important?

Day 17

Read 1 Timothy 5:21–25

As Paul's representative and a spiritual shepherd in Ephesus, Timothy had many responsibilities. Paul has already carefully instructed him on how to guide and minister to the various groups in the church, while being mindful that believers are to conduct themselves in a way that glorifies God and builds up the church. Timothy has to watch his own life and doctrine as well as watch over his flock.

Now, Paul charges Timothy (take note of the times he does this) to "keep these instructions without partiality" (1 Timothy 5:21). The charge is given not only on earth but also in the sight and presence of God, Jesus, and the angels.

How wonderful it is to remember that all that we say and do is in God's presence. In the highly secularised modern world, we often forget this larger picture. In many ways, that which is unseen is more real, significant, and longlasting than that which is seen (2 Corinthians 4:18). How aware are we of this unseen presence of God in our worship services and during all other times?

Timothy is given further instructions. He is not to practise favouritism (1 Timothy 5:21), for this would result in abuse and complaints. A pastor will lose his integrity if he favours only certain groups in church. Timothy must be impartial in keeping Paul's instructions and show no favouritism in his relationships with church members.

Also, he should take care when selecting leaders (1 Timothy 3:1–13). He should "not be hasty in the laying on of hands" (referring to ordination or commissioning; 1 Timothy 5:22). How much damage can be done in church because of poorly chosen leaders! The ones who choose them have to share the blame and the guilt (5:22).

Spiritual discernment and pastoral wisdom are needed in assessing people. While some show their inner corruption quickly and visibly, others may be able to hide them for a long time (5:24). Likewise, the inner character of people may not be revealed through a hasty assessment (5:25). Spiritual and character formation is a process, and sufficient time must be given to make a careful and prayerful assessment.

The medical advice on taking some wine for stomach problems and other ailments in verse 23 seems to be out of place in the passage. Paul may have included this out of pastoral concern for Timothy and to clarify that "purity" is not inconsistent with taking some wine, which is contrary to the false teaching of asceticism.

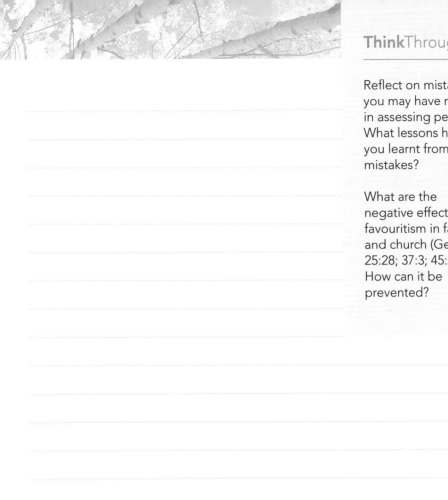

Reflect on mistakes
you may have made
in assessing people.
What lessons have
you learnt from these
mistakes?

What are the
negative effects of
favouritism in family
and church (Genesis
25:28; 37:3; 45:22)?
How can it be
prevented?

Day 18

Read 1 Timothy 6:1–2

The church in Ephesus, like many other churches in the Roman Empire, had a significant number of slaves. This reflected the societies in which the churches were found. There were free men and slaves. Slaves were bonded to their masters and could be given various duties, which included educating the young and administering their masters' household in addition to menial tasks.

For many slaves, it was a difficult life, and they could easily be abused by wicked masters. Paul refers to them in his instructions. They were "under the yoke of slavery" (1 Timothy 6:1). Slaves would very much want to be freed from this bondage.

What happens when a slave becomes a Christian? Paul's instructions are clear in verse 1: **Christian slaves must show Christ-likeness by giving their masters "full respect".** They must not rebel or take shortcuts in their work. If their masters are wicked men, perhaps they may be converted through the testimony and lives of their Christian slaves one day. If their masters are not believers, Christian slaves must behave and serve in such a way that "God's name and our teaching may not be slandered" (6:1).

Should the church not fight against slavery and act to free slaves?

Thankfully, this was done later in history, through the efforts of people like English politician William Wilberforce. But why was Paul not radical enough in acting against slavery? Perhaps it was because of how deeply slavery was entrenched in society. Sudden and forced changes would not be possible or advisable, as they could provoke violence.

At the same time, Paul does condemn those who were involved in slave trading (1 Timothy 1:10), such as slave dealers and kidnappers who would steal the slaves of others and sell them. He also advises Christian slave owners to treat their slaves differently, perhaps even freeing them (Philemon).

Individual slaves are to serve in an exemplary way and not bring disrepute to the gospel through disruptive or disobedient behaviour. Some Christian slaves who had Christian masters might have been presumptuous and might have treated them with "disrespect" (1 Timothy 6:2), meaning they took advantage of their masters by compromising their quality of service. Paul argues that, in this case, though they may not have the fear that other slaves have under wicked masters, they should be motivated by love to serve their Christian masters just as well, if not better.

ThinkThrough

What modern forms of slavery are there today? What should be the church's response to them?

Think of the principles behind Paul's instructions to Christian slaves. How can these be missed, misunderstood, or wrongly applied?

Day 19

Read 1 Timothy 6:3–5

Paul returns to the issues he raised at the beginning of the letter. He reiterates the danger of false teachers because of the harm they do in church.

False teachers teach things that are not in line with "the sound instruction of our Lord Jesus Christ and to godly teaching" (1 Timothy 6:3). Their heretical teachings do not flow from the Lord's teachings and are in opposition to the apostles' teachings. We can determine this by checking what they say against Scripture (Acts 17:11).

The *knowledge* of false teachers is seriously deficient. They "understand nothing" (1 Timothy 6:4). Like blind guides, they will lead people astray—and this is dangerous if you are trying to avoid the way of death and find the way of life.

The *character* of false teachers is corrupt. They are greedy, thinking "that godliness is a means to financial gain" (v. 5). They turn their ministry into a business and mislead people into thinking that it pays materially to be godly. Modern versions of the "health and wealth gospel" exemplify such distorted teaching. Because heresy can be attractive, heretics can find it to be a lucrative business opportunity when misled people happily support them.

The *focus* of false teachers is unhelpful and harmful. "They have an unhealthy interest in controversies and quarrels about words" (v. 4). Their main intention is not to lead people to God by teaching life-giving words, but to show how clever they are. Being attention seekers, they become adept at religious showmanship, using debating skills and oratory to bring glory to themselves. They are like "quack" doctors who, instead of giving patients the right medicine for their potentially fatal illnesses, give lectures on the merits of eating apples rather than oranges!

The *fruit* of false teachers' ministry will speak for itself. They will damage the church by causing "envy, strife, malicious talk, evil suspicions and constant friction" (vv. 4–5). The false teachers will produce more ungodliness, create strong divisions, and allow sin to reign in the church. "Robbed of the truth" (v. 5), they will rob the church of its harmony and godliness. **The church must beware of such false teachers.**

Why do you think heresy can look exciting and attractive? Consider the latest trends in academia and popular culture towards ancient heresies (e.g. *The Da Vinci Code*).

What do you think would characterise "sound instruction" (1 Timothy 6:3)? Who are models of such teaching (authors, preachers, and teachers in church)? How can you encourage them?

Day 20

Read 1 Timothy 6:6–10

When someone is placing portions of food on your plate, they may ask you to "Say when" to indicate when to stop. If you are greedy or wasteful, you may take your time to say it.

When God sent manna from heaven as food for the Israelites, He wanted them to "gather enough for that day" (Exodus 16:4). People gathered different amounts but their daily portions were just what they needed; food kept for the next day became rotten (16:18–20). And those who went out to gather food on the Sabbath found none, having already gathered twice as much the previous day (16:22, 27).

The lessons learnt in the desert were easily forgotten in the marketplace. Paul describes "those who want to get rich" (1 Timothy 6:9). They faced many dangers to their souls. They were not contented with what they already had (which was more than enough), but wanted more and more. What drove them was "the love of money" (6:10), which is the "root of all kinds of evil".

Money itself is not the problem, for many devout Christians have used their wealth for the work of God and to help the poor (Luke 8:3; Acts 4:36–37, 16:14–15). The problem is greed—wanting and keeping more than we need in a way that erodes our souls. **Money can be a potent instrument to be used for the good of others, but it can also overpower us and become our master. It can become our god.**

Jesus warned about the foolishness of trying to serve both God and money (Matthew 6:24). Many of the false teachers in Ephesus were, in fact, serving money through their greedy schemes (1 Timothy 6:5).

The true servant of God must be marked by contentment rather than greed. It is enough to be godly and contented (6:6–8). The greedy invite temptation ("foolish and harmful desires") and can be entrapped in a process that ends in "ruin and destruction" (v. 9). They can lose their faith and hurt themselves terribly (v. 10). It is best to guard our hearts against greed by steadying our lives with simple gratitude for what we have received from God, and by trusting in Him continually.

What forms of
greed are promoted
and encouraged
in the modern
marketplace?
How do Christians
fare amid such
temptations?
How much do you
really need in
order to live a
contented life?

How can the love
of money make
people wander from
the faith? What
should the church
teach Christians
about greed, the
love of money,
and Christian
contentment?

Day 21

Read 1 Timothy 6:11–12

What do we use our energy for? Life has its many challenges, but it is important to focus our attention and energies on a few things. Here, Paul uses two key verbs: flee and pursue. They represent one of Paul's favourite perspectives on the Christian life (see 2 Timothy 2:22).

Timothy is to flee with all his energy (literally "run for his life") from those things that threaten his soul (1 Timothy 6:10). False doctrine, meaningless teachings or diversions, the love of money—these are some things he must resolutely run away from, like the way Joseph fled from Potiphar's wife and her temptations (Genesis 39:12).

The Ten Commandments have many commands that are set in the negative form: "Do not . . ." This has led some people to have the wrong idea of godliness.

The Pharisees were an example: their whole religion was built on a framework of how to avoid breaking the Law. Therefore, in order not to flout the Sabbath law, they devised all kinds of human rules to define what constituted work on the Sabbath. In the process, they failed to show compassion for the sick and needy, and accused Jesus of breaking the Sabbath when He healed people (Matthew 12:9–14). Jesus had to teach His listeners that the whole Law and the Prophets can be summarised in the two commandments: love God and love your neighbour (Matthew 22:37–40).

Godliness consists of both fleeing from evil and pursuing good. While Timothy must flee from sin and evil, he must also pursue with all his energy those things that will glorify God (1 Timothy 6:11). He must pursue wholehearted devotion to God (godliness), holiness in relationships (righteousness), trust in God (faith), selfless relationships (love), and bearing with difficult circumstances (endurance) and people (gentleness) so that in all these things, Christ-likeness would be revealed.

The twin ideas of fleeing and pursuing are further reiterated by the terms "fight" and "take hold" in 1 Timothy 6:12. "Fight the good fight" is a favourite metaphor of Paul (1 Timothy 1:18; 2 Timothy 4:7). "Take hold of the eternal life" (to which Paul and Timothy were called) conveys the idea of a firm grasp of the Christian identity (see Timothy's public confession), heritage, and destiny.

What must you currently flee from? What new areas would you include in your list? How well are you doing on this front?

Likewise, how well are you pursuing some of the qualities or virtues listed by Paul? Consider other virtues or habits. How can the phrases "fight the good fight" and "take hold of the eternal life" motivate you in your pursuit of godliness?

Day 22

Read 1 Timothy 6:13–16

I n *The Great House of God*, author Max Lucado relates what sociologists observed about mountain climbers. There was a connection between clouds in the sky and contentment in the hearts of climbers. If the mountain peak was visible, the climbers were energetic and cooperative. If it was hidden by cloud cover, they were sulky and selfish.

Paul says the same thing to Timothy. He encourages Timothy to keep his eyes on "the King of kings and Lord of lords" (1 Timothy 6:15). **The greatness of God is deeply inspiring and life giving.** He alone is immortal and lives in unapproachable light (6:16). He is so glorious and unique that no one has seen or can see Him. But He has revealed himself through His Son Jesus Christ (Colossians 1:15; Hebrews 1:1–3), who testified to His glorious identity before Pontius Pilate (1 Timothy 6:13; see John 18:33–37).

In the midst of sorting out problems and discharging his pastoral duties in the church, Timothy must keep his eyes on the heavenly peaks of God's nature and promises. By looking at the "only Ruler" of heaven and earth (which means God is sovereign and in control of all things), Timothy will have a spring in his step no matter how difficult the road. His anticipation of "the appearing of our Lord Jesus, which God will bring about in his own time" (1 Timothy 6:14–15), will help him bear present burdens, no matter how heavy and tiresome.

Paul encourages and fortifies Timothy by delivering another charge in the presence of this majestic and awesome God and His Son our Saviour (6:13): Timothy must remember that God is the Divine Witness and Ultimate Observer who is watching everything. He knows every situation and every person. Nothing escapes His notice.

Because Timothy's calling came from Almighty God, and because he lives and serves in God's presence, Timothy is to fulfil all his duties "without spot or blame" (6:14). He must be full of faith and faithfulness as he makes himself fully available to God to such an extent that his life and ministry will be full of divine grace and power, being marked with integrity and effectiveness.

What happens to us when we lose sight of God's greatness, purposes, and promises? What can you do to avoid being so overwhelmed by "the mess" on the ground that you forget the Messiah in heaven?

If God is the only Ruler, what are the implications? How should this affect our emotions, attitudes, perspectives, relationships, and choices?

Day 23

Read 1 Timothy 6:17–19

John Wesley was used by God to lead a revival movement in 17th-century Britain and America. Near the end of his life, he worried about the Methodists. He reflected on the cycle that all revivals go through—holiness is revived, people live frugally, then they become wealthy, and subsequently they become arrogant and lose their zeal. The Methodists were becoming wealthier and Wesley prayed over how they could be taught not to lose their original fervour.

Many churches have their fair share of "those who are rich in this present world" (1 Timothy 6:17). Through hard work or favourable personal circumstances, they have more than they need. Herein lies a spiritual danger: the more we have, the less we tend to feel the need for God. The danger of becoming arrogant (6:17) is always there when we think that what we have is due to our own smartness or effort (Deuteronomy 8:11–14,17–18).

Paul instructs Timothy to command two things of the rich. Firstly, they must put their hope in God and not in their wealth (1 Timothy 6:17). Someone once referred to the phrase "In God we trust" printed on American dollar bills, and wondered which god it really refers to. Money can easily become the god that people trust, but it is unreliable and "uncertain" (6:17). Instead, rich Christians must put their hope in the right place. They are rich because God is rich, and it is He "who richly provides us with everything for our enjoyment" (6:17). We must never forget the hand that feeds us (Psalm 104:28, 145:16; Matthew 6:26).

Secondly, rich Christians must be "generous and willing to share" (1 Timothy 6:18). Many rich people are poor givers. Wesley came up with a solution to this predicament. He taught the Methodists to "earn all you can, save all you can, give all you can". Hard work and frugality must be matched with generosity. The early church demonstrated this, and "there was no needy person among them" (Acts 4:34).

There are always people poorer than us. How about sharing what we have with them? **Our wealth is not measured by what we keep for ourselves, but by what we give away to those in need.** In this way Christians will "lay up treasure for themselves as a firm foundation for the coming age" (1 Timothy 6:19; see Matthew 6:19–21).

Why does the church still have needy people? How can there be a better and more caring re-distribution of wealth in the church and society?

Paul urges Timothy to "take hold of the life that is truly life" (1 Timothy 6:19). What do you think he had in mind? Reflect on the words of Jesus in John 10:10.

Day 24

Read 1 Timothy 6:20–21

n bringing his first epistle to Timothy to an end, Paul reiterates his earlier points by focusing on two verbs.

Firstly, Timothy must "turn away" from false knowledge, bad doctrine, and those things that do not contribute to godliness (1 Timothy 6:20).

Bad doctrine presents itself in attractive ways. In Ephesus, it came in the guise of "knowledge". It was fashionable for philosophers and travelling teachers to tout their philosophies and exotic and mysterious knowledge. The false teachers in Ephesus were doing the same, offering knowledge that amounted to nothing in the end. It was nothing more than "godless chatter" (v. 20). In fact, such useless knowledge was spiritually dangerous because it often led people astray. Christians who swallowed all of it hook, line, and sinker had "departed from the faith" (v. 21). In attaining such "knowledge", they had lost their life-giving faith in Christ.

The measure of any teaching is not how attractive and tantalising it is, but how true it is. Its truth will always be measured by what Scripture teaches.

False teaching may be more popular and attract bigger crowds, but faithful servants of God must never allow themselves to be tempted to change course or waver in the way they hold on to sound teaching. As a faithful pastor, Timothy needs to set a good example to his flock.

The second verb is "guard". With the same energy employed in turning away from the allure of false teaching, Timothy must guard what had been entrusted to him—namely the gospel of Jesus Christ. He must hold on to it in his preaching, defend it in his teaching, and propagate it in his ministry. To do so, Timothy must remain vigilant, watching not only his own thoughts and teachings, but also what was being taught in church by others, including what believers were discussing among themselves.

Timothy, in turning away and in guarding, would be a faithful servant of God and a trustworthy pastor whom God would use to build His church. Timothy wouldn't be able to do this on his own strength, but by divine grace (v. 21).

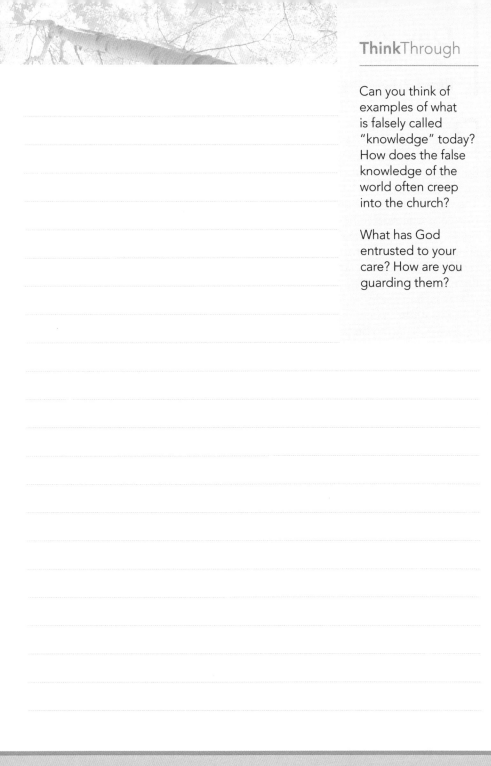

ThinkThrough

Can you think of examples of what is falsely called "knowledge" today? How does the false knowledge of the world often creep into the church?

What has God entrusted to your care? How are you guarding them?

Day 25

Read 2 Timothy 1:1–4

Paul's final epistle, 2 Timothy, was written two years after 1 Timothy. It was written from a prison cell in Rome, just before Paul's martyrdom.

The wicked and mad Roman emperor Nero was believed to have set fire to Rome. He blamed Christians for the fire and had many Christians arrested, tortured, and killed by wrapping them in pitched clothes, tying them to stakes, and setting them on fire to light the streets. Amid this mayhem, Paul was waiting to be tried in court. He knew he was likely to be killed (2 Timothy 4:6). Therefore, he writes to his favourite protégé Timothy, sharing his final thoughts.

Two things can be noted in these opening verses. Firstly, Paul's strong sense of identity and calling. **Paul was clear that he served the living God, the God of his forefathers.** He was not a fly-by-night preacher who had turned up out of nowhere. His identity was deeply rooted in his rich heritage: the long history of his people, and God's relationship with them. The God he served was the same God his forefathers served (2 Timothy 1:3). The gospel was firmly rooted in the

history of his people. Jesus is the Lion of Judah; the Son of David; a Branch from Jesse; and the promised Messiah.

Again, Paul emphasises serving God with a clear conscience (v. 3). He had got it wrong, of course, before his conversion. But he had served with all seriousness and sincerity. After meeting Jesus, he knew better and all the more served God wholeheartedly and with great zeal. He was convinced of the "promise of life that is in Christ Jesus" (v. 1)—that eternal life comes through Jesus. For this reason, he was called to be an apostle; this was not his own choice, but God's will.

Secondly, we note Paul's fatherly relationship with Timothy. He addresses Timothy as "my dear son" (v. 2). He might have personally brought Timothy to a saving knowledge of Christ. He certainly discipled the younger man. He prays for Timothy "night and day" (v. 3) as he remembers Timothy's tears when they last parted company (v. 4). He longs to see his spiritual son again before he dies. These expressions speak of how deeply Paul loves Timothy.

Review Paul's
calling (Acts 9:15–16,
22:14–15, 26:17–18).
How do you think
Paul's experience
of being called by
God so specifically
and clearly helped
him in his difficult
circumstances?

Paul constantly
remembered
Timothy in his
prayers. What do
you think Paul would
have prayed about
for Timothy? Who
are the people you
need to pray for in
the same way?

Day 26

Read 2 Timothy 1:5–7

Paul was strong, tenacious, and tough. Timothy, on the other hand, was timid (2 Timothy 1:7). He was not so confident and was perhaps afraid of people. Such timidity would be a disadvantage in Christian leadership. Paul encourages Timothy by reminding him of two truths.

Firstly, Timothy must remember his great heritage. Paul had already mentioned his own heritage and calling. Timothy had a Jewish mother (Eunice) and a Greek father (Acts 16:1). As such, he already shared Paul's heritage. In addition, Timothy had strong family role models. He would have been inspired by his godly grandmother Lois and mother. They both became believers, but even before that, as devout Jews, they would have taught Timothy the Scriptures (2 Timothy 3:15). Their sincere faith was transferred to Timothy (1:5).

When life becomes painful and unbearable, it is often helpful to remember those who have inspired and nurtured us, those who believe in us, and those who are praying for us. This is why prisoners of war often remember their families and find new comfort and strength. Therefore, Paul urged Timothy to remember his heritage.

Secondly, Timothy must remember his calling and spiritual enablement. Paul and the body of elders laid hands on Timothy at his ordination (2 Timothy 1:6; 1 Timothy 4:14). Not only was a prophetic message given, but "a gift of God" (2 Timothy 1:6) was also imparted to Timothy. This gift could refer to the Holy Spirit or to a particular gifting for ministry. Whatever the case might have been, Timothy ought to remember that God himself had called and equipped him adequately for his pastoral task. The gift of God was in him. He should draw strength from this fact and overcome his timidity.

The "power" (1:7) that Timothy had received should make him resilient and strong. However, some people misunderstand spiritual power and explain it in terms of worldly power—which can be arrogant, bossy, bullying, and even abusive and violent. True spiritual power is always connected with divine love and human self-discipline (1:7). As John Calvin said, "The powerful energy of the Spirit is tempered by love and soberness."

How will you thank God for the great heritage you have as a Christian? Think of biblical characters, Christians in history, and those you know personally.

What do you think Paul had in mind when he urged Timothy to "fan into flame the gift of God" (2 Timothy 1:6)? What personal implications are there for you?

Day 27

Read 2 Timothy 1:8–10

We are now entering the glorious truth of the gospel. It is centred on God's eternal purposes in Christ. Paul refers to the *grace of God*, which "was given us in Christ Jesus before the beginning of time" (2 Timothy 1:9). This is an amazing truth—God's gracious dealing with us originated before anything in this universe existed. The point is that there is nothing in our actions or in this world that can save us. We are saved entirely by the grace of God. This timeless grace of God has now been revealed in history through Christ.

He appeared on earth through His incarnation, died on the cross for us, and rose victoriously from death. He "destroyed death" and "brought life and immortality to light" (v. 10). It is through this Jesus that God has "saved us and called us to a holy life" according to "his own purpose and grace" (v. 9). This, in brief, is the gospel of Jesus.

To declare this gospel to an unfriendly world that persecuted and killed its messengers was a daunting task. Here, Paul introduces the *power of God*.

This power that operated in Jesus is also at work when people are saved and made holy. It is also present in the messengers of the gospel. Timid Timothy, who had received the power of God, must therefore take heart amid difficulties. God's power would help him on two counts.

Firstly, he should have courage and "not be ashamed of the testimony about our Lord" (v. 8). People may laugh at the preaching of the gospel (1 Corinthians 1:22–23), but preachers must have a "thick skin" and boldly preach the truth.

Secondly, he should be willing to suffer. The power of God will enable him to do so and give him endurance (Colossians 1:11). Paul was a prisoner on death row. Not many wanted to be associated with someone accused of a crime against the state—it was dangerous. But Paul asks Timothy not to be ashamed of him (2 Timothy 1:8).

The glory of the gospel and the power of God will help us to boldly proclaim God's truth and be willing to suffer.

How precious is the gospel of Christ to you? How do you understand God's grace and power in Christ? What evidence is there that you hold this gospel dear to your heart?

Paul invites Timothy to join him in suffering for the gospel. Why is there comfort in knowing that you are not suffering alone, but there are other fellow believers who similarly suffer for the gospel?

Day 28

Read 2 Timothy 1:11–12

Paul suffered much while faithfully serving the Lord. He knew that his suffering arose because he was loyal to the Lord. He could have easily compromised his message (watering it down) and his methods (taking the politically correct route). But it was better to be faithful and suffer for it, than to be unfaithful and enjoy comfort and a false peace.

The Lord appointed Paul to the gospel ministry (2 Timothy 1:11). His role was that of a herald (gospel preacher), apostle (missionary and appointed leader), and teacher (one who fed God's flock with God's truth). He proclaimed the gospel boldly, led with integrity, and taught diligently and faithfully. Now he was in prison and branded as an enemy of the state. Many avoided him to stay out of trouble. The great apostle was chained like an animal. Yet, Paul was not ashamed (v. 12). There is no shame greater than the shame Jesus suffered for us in the humiliation of the cross. The next time you are humiliated for being loyal to Jesus, let Jesus look you in the eye to comfort and cheer you.

This brings us to the heart of Paul's resilience and hope amid great difficulties. His relationship with Jesus was the solid foundation and anchor of his life and ministry. He declares, "I know whom I have believed" (v. 12). Three things can be noted here.

First, *trust*. Paul believed in Jesus. He placed his faith in Jesus more than in anything or anyone else.

Second, *intimacy*. Paul had a close personal relationship with Jesus. He was familiar with the way the Lord was present every day, and with how He answered prayers, guided, protected, and provided for needs. Jesus was more than a doctrine or concept. Paul knew Him as a Person.

Third, *confidence*. Because he knew Jesus and trusted Him, Paul had unshakeable confidence that Jesus would guard what Paul had entrusted to Him for the final day (v. 12; see 1 Peter 4:19). **All that we entrust into the hands of the Lord (our lives, our future, and the results of our ministry) will remain safe with Jesus.** No one can snatch us from His hands (John 10:28–30).

Reflect on the trust, intimacy, and confidence that marked Paul's relationship with Jesus. How would you characterise your relationship with Jesus?

Verse 12 in the original Greek can also mean that Jesus will guard that which He had entrusted to Paul, namely the gospel. If so, what comfort did that bring to Paul then and to you now?

Day 29

Read 2 Timothy 1:13–14

The gospel that God had entrusted to Paul was in turn entrusted to Timothy. Paul refers to "what you heard from me" (2 Timothy 1:13). This is the "pattern of sound teaching"—the body of doctrines that conveyed the gospel of Jesus Christ. This originated from Christ, who taught from the Scriptures, and He passed it on to His apostles. This apostolic teaching had a certain "pattern" that was to be guarded and passed on faithfully (v. 13). We note that this "good deposit" is not only "sound" but can also be passed on from one person to another, and from one generation to another (vv. 13–14).

The early church was infiltrated by false teachers and heresy. They were teaching "a different gospel" (Galatians 1:6–7), a perverted one contrary to the true gospel of Jesus Christ. It was important that the integrity of the gospel was guarded against such challenges. Timothy was to guard and entrust the gospel to others faithfully (2 Timothy 2:2).

Guarding the gospel should take the form of resisting false teaching, faithfully teaching the "sound teaching" of God's revealed truth, and watching your own life to avoid compromise and falling into apostasy. In short, "watch your life and doctrine" (1 Timothy 4:16).

Entrusting requires that we choose carefully those who will continue the gospel ministry. God had carefully entrusted the gospel to Paul. Paul had entrusted the same to Timothy. It would be necessary for Timothy to pass on the gospel to others who could be trusted (2 Timothy 2:2). What is important here is the trust that is involved. Such trust takes time to develop in a relationship. We must be concerned not only about what happens during our watch, but also what will follow. We must not be like King Hezekiah who, when told that the palace would be raided in the future, was selfishly satisfied that there would be peace during his rule (Isaiah 39:5–8).

A certain church leader put it this way: "A leader must not drop things, but pass them on faithfully." The baton must be passed from hand to hand without being lost. We cannot do this in our own strength, but with the help of the Holy Spirit (2 Timothy 1:14). He helps us from above and from within, for He dwells in us. His help is always available.

Reflect on the "good deposit" that has been entrusted to you. Who have been your mentors (past and present, living and dead)? How are you guarding this deposit?

How does the Holy Spirit help us to guard the "good deposit" both as individuals and as a church? What difference does it make to have the Spirit living in us?

Day 30

Read 2 Timothy 1:15–18

t is not easy to see your friends desert you when you need them most. Paul realised that some of his close associates had run away when he was charged with treason and locked up in prison, awaiting a trial that would inevitably end in a death sentence. They were "ashamed" of Paul and also afraid of getting into trouble. Like Peter, who denied having anything to do with Jesus when the Lord was arrested (Luke 22:54–62), they distanced themselves from Paul.

Paul had taught in Ephesus for around two years, and "all the Jews and Greeks who lived in the province of Asia heard the word of the Lord" (Acts 19:10). All Asia had heard the gospel and many believed. Now, however, all Asia had deserted Paul. He said, "everyone in the province of Asia has deserted me" (2 Timothy 1:15).

Two men received special mention: Phygelus and Hermogenes (v. 15). The reason is that these two were least expected to turn tail and run away. As American New Testament scholar Robert Mounce puts it, "It was as if Paul is saying, 'Even these two faithful brethren have deserted me in my hour of need'." They had lost their courage, which comes from the Holy Spirit.

Thankfully, Paul was not totally abandoned. He is full of praise for Onesiphorus (vv. 16–18), who was neither ashamed of Paul's chains nor afraid to be associated with Paul. He was one of Paul's associates (having helped Paul in Ephesus, v. 18) who had travelled to Rome to find his friend.

In those days, prisoners had to find their own food and supplies to survive. Onesiphorus probably brought with him some much-needed supplies for Paul. He must have faced considerable difficulty searching throughout the unfamiliar city for Paul (v. 17). What a joy it must have been for Paul to see him. He was "like a breath of fresh air" (v. 16, TLB). He must have visited Paul often, and probably died (or was killed because of his close association with Paul, the political prisoner) during this time. Here was a faithful friend who stuck till the end, who literally gave his life for his friend (see John 15:13).

Imagine how Paul must have felt when he heard that many of his close friends had abandoned or disowned him, proving themselves to be fair-weather friends. If you were in Paul's place, how would you respond or pray for such people?

How do you think Onesiphorus "refreshed" (2 Timothy 1:16) Paul in prison? Can you think of anyone who needs to be refreshed in this way—in a prison, hospital, nursing home, and so on? What can you do to help?

Read 2 Timothy 2:1–2

In 1 Timothy, Paul had given instructions to Timothy on the qualifications of overseers. They must be exemplary in their character and effective in their primary ministry of teaching. Here, the same points are reiterated for Timothy to apply in his own life—both what he should *be* and what he should *do*.

Timothy is urged to "be strong" (2 Timothy 2:1). We are reminded of how Joshua was also repeatedly urged to be strong as he assumed leadership before the conquest of Canaan (Joshua 1:7, 9, 18). The task was extremely difficult, but God was with him and promised him success.

Likewise, Timothy is urged to be strong amid the difficult circumstances of his ministry. He was timid by nature, but God would give him supernatural strength according to the difficulty of the task. This strength that comes from God is "in the grace that is in Christ Jesus" (2 Timothy 2:1). We can pray and trust God for such strength. As clergyman Phillips Brooks advised, "Do not pray for tasks equal to your powers. Pray for powers equal to your tasks."

Timothy is also urged to "entrust to reliable people who will also be qualified to teach others" (v. 2). He had received the gospel and the apostolic teaching from Paul. Now he must pass on what he had received and learned.

We see here a living stream in which the gospel is passed on faithfully from one generation of leaders and teachers to the next. Paul received it and passed it to Timothy. Timothy is to do the same with others he is mentoring. He must ensure that they too would do the same. The gospel is like an Olympic flame or baton that is passed on from one runner to the next. Every teacher must ensure that he is not the weakest link in this chain. He can do this by relying on the grace of Christ to be strong, so that he will not drop the baton because of fear, distraction, or fatigue.

In summary, Paul urges Timothy to be strong and to be faithful in his teaching and mentoring ministry. This combination of God-given inner strength and diligent ministry that continues from generation to generation is illustrated in the three metaphors that Paul uses in the next passage.

What are the differences between man-made strength and God-given strength? Can you recall instances when you experienced how "God [was] the strength of [your] heart" (Psalm 73:26)? Why is God's strength needed to do God's work?

Who are the "Pauls" in your life who have entrusted the gospel and the truths of God to you? Who are the "Timothys" to whom you must entrust what you have received? How can this ongoing mentoring process be strengthened in the church?

Read 2 Timothy 2:3–4

Godly inner strength and faithful ministry can be seen in the three metaphors Paul uses. Firstly, Timothy is to be like a devoted and faithful soldier. Soldiering was one of Paul's favourite metaphors to describe the Christian life and its challenges (1 Corinthians 9:7; 2 Corinthians 10:3–6; Ephesians 6:10–18; 1 Timothy 6:12; Philippians 2:25).

Being a soldier is not easy, as any military recruit discovers in boot camp. During training, soldiers are stretched to the limits and put through various trials, knowing that actual war is even worse. Soldiers can suffer much hardship, but they have to endure such deprivation and suffering if they don't want to become deserters. Paul urges Timothy, "Join with me in suffering, like a good soldier of Christ Jesus" (2 Timothy 2:3). Paul was a veteran soldier of Christ. He was like "an iron pillar" (Jeremiah 1:18), "hard pressed on every side, but not crushed" (2 Corinthians 4:8).

Timothy could draw courage and comfort from the fact that he was not a lone soldier on the battlefield. Instead, he was part of a great company of faithful and courageous soldiers of Christ whose only desire was to please Christ, their "commanding officer" (2 Timothy 2:4). They were totally devoted to Christ their King.

Good soldiers don't get involved in civilian affairs (2:4). They are so focused on soldiering that they will not allow any distractions in their lives. In the spiritual life, you cannot be a part-time soldier of Christ. The battle can take place at any time or all the time (Ephesians 6:10–18). Satan is like a roaring lion, a master at ambushing Christians (1 Peter 5:8).

But the metaphor of full-time soldiering does not mean that all Christians should become monks or priests. Reformer Martin Luther insisted that we must faithfully serve in the stations that God has placed us—whether as farmers, doctors, teachers, or salespersons. What is important is that we should be very focused on devoting ourselves to Christ and serving Him, so that in all things we will bring Him glory (1 Corinthians 10:31).

Whatever our job or role in life, French theologian John Calvin's assertion is relevant: "Everyone who wishes to fight under Christ's command must relinquish all the trifles and diversions of this world and devote all his energies to the fight."

Remembering that our weapons are not of this world (2 Corinthians 10:4), why do you think soldiers of Christ must be prepared to endure much hardship? How can they find help in such circumstances?

Devotion and focus are key ideas in Paul's metaphor regarding soldiers. How would you assess your own devotion to Christ? How are you focusing on the tasks He has given you?

Day 33

Read 2 Timothy 2:5

The second metaphor is that of a disciplined athlete. Paul draws his example from the popular Olympian and Isthmian Games. Winners were held in high regard because their victory was the result of hard and disciplined training. The Christian life is like an athletic race or wrestling match (1 Timothy 6:12; 2 Timothy 4:7–8; 1 Corinthians 9:24–27; Philippians 3:13–14; Hebrews 12:1). It requires the right motive, habits, and values.

Christians must run the race in order to win (1 Corinthians 9:24). There is no point in competing if all they can produce is a half-hearted attempt. Christians must be serious about following Christ and becoming holy through the sanctifying work of the Holy Spirit. The standards set by Jesus are exacting—we cannot be His disciples if we are not willing to give Him everything (Luke 14:26–27, 33). We are to spare no effort in pursuing Christ, so that we can grow in our knowledge of Him and not be ineffective and unproductive (2 Peter 1:5–8). Good athletes run to win and to give their best.

Athletes of Christ must also train hard (1 Corinthians 9:25). They must have disciplined habits. They do not take holidays from training. Paul mentions the fact that no athlete in the Games would be able to win the victor's crown "except by competing according to the rules" (2 Timothy 2:5). Scholars believe that this could refer to the rule in the Greek Games that all athletes must have trained for 10 months to qualify as participants. There were no shortcuts. Disciplined training was necessary to run the race.

The rules could also refer to the kind that is necessary in sports. Breaking such rules would bring disqualification. Therefore, the athlete must keep to the rules of the sport. For the Christian, this means that the Christian life cannot be lived without obeying God's rules. Christian ministry must also be conducted according to divine rules and principles.

In summary, like the highly disciplined athlete, the Christian should have the proper motive (an all-out desire to win the race), habits (of disciplined training and practice), and value system (high regard for God's laws and rules, and faithful obedience to them). There is no place for half-hearted attempts and incomplete races.

How can you ensure that the motivation to win comes not from the sinful ambition of the flesh, but from the zeal of the Lord given by the Holy Spirit?

What are some biblical rules which if ignored or broken, would cause the spiritual race to be lost? What are some disciplined habits that will help you to complete and win the race?

Day 34

Read 2 Timothy 2:6–7

Paul's third metaphor is that of a diligent farmer. The "hardworking farmer" is the first to receive a share of the harvest (2 Timothy 2:6). Lazy or negligent farmers cannot have good harvests.

Farming is not an easy occupation (this was especially true in Paul's day). Farmers have to exercise great discipline and diligence in waking early every day to tend to their crops and farm their animals. Ploughing, planting, weeding, watering, feeding, and so on can be tiring. These are thankless tasks at the time, but they bring fruit and harvest in due course. As such, farmers must be not only hardworking, but also patient. Crops do not grow overnight. If people are impatient, they cannot be farmers.

We live in an industrialised modern era where speed and instant gratification are part of everyday life. In spiritual matters, however, progress is made at a pace that is often closer to the slower, gradual process that is seen in agricultural cultivation, rather than the speed of mechanised factory production or ease of supermarket shopping. Many Christians make the error of measuring their spiritual growth by modern standards. They need to learn the ways of the farmer.

The Lord's field is in the heart (personal discipleship), church (Christian nurture), and world (mission and evangelism). It is imperative that we give regular attention to this field and not just rely on occasional spurts of action. Like the hardworking farmer, daily and diligent input is required. New Testament scholar N. T. Wright's wise advice is apt: "Beware of the temptation to engage in the Christian life like a kind of absentee landlord, expecting the benefits without having to do any of the hard work."

Having put forth his three striking metaphors, Paul calls Timothy to "reflect on what I am saying" (2:7). He assures the younger pastor that the Lord will give him the necessary insight. Here is a wonderful union of God's grace and our response to it. We must take time to reflect on God's Word, and God will do the rest. Divine illumination comes with our diligent effort to study God's Word and our serious reflection on it.

Anglican bishop J. C. Ryle wrote: "There are no spiritual gains without pains." Why is hard work necessary to have a rich harvest?

Spiritual comprehension comes to the person who prayerfully reflects on God's truths. What does this say about making a regular habit of Bible reading and prayer?

Day 35

Read 2 Timothy 2:8–10

Remembering is important in Christian discipleship. Servants, for example, must remember their master's parting instructions in order to be found faithfully carrying them out when the master returns suddenly (Matthew 24:45–51). Likewise, we must remember Jesus Christ (2 Timothy 2:8). We must fix our eyes on Jesus in order to run the race with perseverance (Hebrews 12:2).

Paul describes Jesus as "raised from the dead" and "descended from David" (2 Timothy 2:8). Each description says something vitally important about Jesus. Jesus is both fully divine (proven by His miraculous resurrection) and fully human (being a human descendant of King David); He is both the Son of God and the son of David. This is a reiteration of what Paul had written to the Romans (Romans 1:1–4). The apostle John referred to Jesus as "the only begotten God" (John 1:18 NASB).

In the early church (and even today), heresies developed when either the divinity or the humanity of Jesus was denied. The Bible holds both facts together (Matthew 1:20–21; Luke 1:35; John 1:14; 1 John 1:1–4); reflection on this truth will help us to understand the nature of the triune God and His

eternal purposes to save us. Paul calls this declaration "my gospel" (2 Timothy 2:8), for which he was suffering—"being chained like a criminal" (v. 9). The truth about Jesus and His gospel is worth enduring any amount of suffering.

Paul reflected on his chains in prison while probably dictating 2 Timothy to his friend Luke (4:11). He must have smiled when saying, "But God's word is not chained" (2:9). You can imprison the messenger, but you cannot imprison God's Word! Paul was comforted by the power of God's Word and the failure of human and demonic attempts to suppress or snuff out the gospel. The truth of Jesus cannot be quashed because God will not allow that. God, who is out to save those whom He has predestined ("the elect" in 2:10), will see to it that Jesus is remembered well so that He can be believed and trusted.

For this reason, Paul was willing to "endure everything" (2:10). Even in chains he was filled with joy as he thought about Jesus and considered himself to be privileged to serve his wonderful Lord.

Why do you think it is heresy to deny either the divinity or the humanity of Christ? Why is the truth that Jesus is both fully divine and fully human necessary for us to understand what He accomplished on the cross for us?

2 Timothy 2:8–10 refers to the deep remembering of Jesus and the tough resilience associated with it. How can we remember Jesus at the Lord's Table (1 Corinthians 11:23–25) so that we can endure everything for the sake of His gospel?

Read 2 Timothy 2:11–13

The "trustworthy saying" (2 Timothy 2:11) that Paul quotes here is a quatrain (a series of four statements) that was probably taken from an early Christian hymn. These statements say something about the nature of the Christian life, the reality of suffering, the danger of apostasy, and the ultimate triumph of Christ.

The first statement ("If we died with him, we will also live with him"; 2:11) refers to our conversion and baptismal experience (see Romans 6:8). We entrust ourselves to Christ by dying to the self and finding new life in Him. This is the secret of the victorious Christian life. For Paul, this truth would have had additional significance. He was about to die for Christ and experience eternal life with his Lord.

The second sentence ("if we endure, we will also reign with him"; 2 Timothy 2:12) points to the suffering that is often a part of the Christian life. But such suffering is nothing compared to the glory of reigning with Christ. "For our light and momentary troubles are achieving for us an eternal glory that far outweighs them all" (2 Corinthians 4:17). Cross bearers on earth will become crown wearers in heaven (2 Timothy 4:8; Revelation 2:10).

The third statement ("If we disown him, he will also disown us"; 2 Timothy 2:12) is a warning against apostasy—of not enduring faithfully. We must resist all such temptations by remembering the words of Jesus (Matthew 10:33). We disown the Lord when His lordship is not declared and demonstrated in our lives. This can easily happen when Christians living in a hostile social environment are focused on saving their own skins.

The fourth statement ("if we are faithless, he will remain faithful, for he cannot disown himself"; 2 Timothy 2:13) is more difficult to interpret. It could mean that God (being faithful to His character) will punish unfaithfulness. It could also mean that human unfaithfulness cannot thwart God's purposes. Our ultimate hope is God's faithfulness. The knowledge that God is faithful will help us to remain loyal to Him.

We should not become presumptuous of God's grace.

Instead, we should be willing to follow Christ by denying ourselves, enduring the suffering associated with it, and, by God's grace and power, remaining faithful to Him in all situations.

Reflect on baptism as dying with Christ and rising with Him to new life (Romans 6:5). Why is the death of the self necessary to live the new life?

What are some ways by which Christians disown Jesus and become unfaithful to Him? What can we do to ensure that we do not fall into such temptations and fatal habits?

Day 37

Read 2 Timothy 2:14–15

A good craftsman derives satisfaction and pleasure from doing his best to produce high-quality work. Likewise, the student of God's Word is expected to be a good "worker" who "does not need to be ashamed" (2 Timothy 2:15) of negligent, shoddy, or half-hearted work.

In challenging false teachers whose favourite pastime was "quarrelling about words" (2:14), and in feeding the flock with God's Word, Timothy is to be a diligent student of Scripture. As a careful craftsman, he will be able to warn the false teachers and their fans of the danger of engaging in useless speculation and of carelessly handling Scripture. Such behaviour "only ruins those who listen" (2:14). Three principles can be noted in verse 15 regarding the right handling of Scripture.

Firstly, *preachers are accountable to God*. They present themselves to God before they present themselves to the congregation. They kneel in prayer before they stand at the pulpit. They need to gain God's approval before they can preach. The leaders whose task it is to choose and authorise preachers must discern those whom God has approved. Remembering that they are accountable to God will make preachers conduct their ministry with all seriousness and with fear and trembling (Psalm 119:120).

Secondly, *preachers and teachers must handle God's Word accurately*. The Greek word *orthotomeō* means "to cut straight", the way a farmer cuts a straight line with the plough. The opposite of *orthotomeō* is *astocheō*, meaning "departed" (2 Timothy 2:18). Careless and irresponsible workmen of God's Word stray from the text and lead themselves and their flocks astray. Scottish theologian William Barclay asserts that a good workman of Scripture "correctly handles the word of truth, drives a straight road through the truth and refuses to be lured down pleasant but irrelevant bypaths".

Thirdly, *good workmen of Scripture will do their best*. The Greek word *spoudazō* means "making every effort with haste, eagerness and zeal". There is to be no cutting of corners or laziness. **Good workmen will spare no effort to accurately and clearly present what the scriptural text says and apply it relevantly to everyday life.** They will emphasise what Scripture emphasises and focus on its focus.

These principles are not only for preachers and teachers, but also for all Christians, in whom the Word of God must richly dwell (Colossians 3:16).

Identify some examples of "quarrelling about words" (2 Timothy 2:14). Why is such a practice useless and harmful to listeners and participants? How is this different from guarding the truth?

Reflect on the three principles stated. Which of these needs to be strengthened in the way you handle Scripture?

Read 2 Timothy 2:16–19

Having urged Timothy to be a good workman of Scripture, Paul provides negative and positive examples. The false teachers were not good workmen of Scripture. They were lazy and engaged in "godless chatter" (2 Timothy 2:16). They demonstrated the saying that "empty vessels make the most noise". Paul singles out two such false teachers, Hymenaeus and Philetus (2:17). Hymenaeus is also mentioned in 1 Timothy 1:19–20 as one who had shipwrecked his faith. Not much else is known of Philetus. Both had "departed from the truth" (2 Timothy 2:18).

Their heresy centred on their claim that the resurrection had already taken place (2:18). How they managed to convince their gullible listeners is not clear. Scholars think that while Paul had taught that the giving of the Holy Spirit was a down payment for the future resurrection (Ephesians 1:13–14), these false teachers may have misled people into thinking that the reception of the Holy Spirit completed salvation and was a sign of spiritual resurrection, and that there was no further resurrection.

Such teaching must have caused much confusion among believers and produced unhelpful and even harmful reactions in those who believed this heresy. The need for a bodily resurrection was dismissed. False confidence that they were saved and didn't need to care about holiness any more (licentiousness) was another reaction. They may have stopped praying. They imagined they did not have to suffer, as they connected the reception of the Spirit with a life that was free from suffering. Modern health and wealth gospels are echoes of that ancient heresy.

In short, their faith was destroyed (2 Timothy 2:18). The heresy spread like gangrene (v. 17), and those who were influenced became increasingly ungodly (v. 16).

Paul, in contrast, was a good workman of Scripture. He demonstrates this in verse 19. Unlike the spreading heresy, God's truth is a solid foundation sealed with an inscription that says two things. "The Lord knows those who are his" points to the all-powerful and all-knowing God. "Everyone who confesses the name of the Lord must turn away from wickedness" refers to the human response to divine grace. Our security in Christ and our responsibility to pursue holiness are both emphasised. If one is held without the other, misunderstanding and even heresy will arise. It is so important to be a good workman of Scripture.

Can you think of some examples of godless chatter? Why does such godless chatter lead to apostasy and ungodliness?

Why do you think Paul included both statements (2 Timothy 2:19) as foundational for the Christian life? What would happen if one is emphasised without the other? Reflect on false security and spiritual restlessness.

Day 39

Read 2 Timothy 2:20–21

Still thinking about the damage that false teachers were causing in the church, Paul turns to another metaphor (2 Timothy 2:20). In a large house, there are typically all kinds of household articles. Some are costly, highly valued, and reserved for noble purposes; others are cheaper and used for ignoble purposes. It would be unacceptable to use a golden vessel as a rubbish bin. Likewise, in the church there are true servants and false ones, faithful teachers and charlatans. God will use only those people who are true to Him.

How would Timothy ensure that he was a useful instrument to the Master? The answer is given in verse 21. There are two ideas to be noted here: people who cleanse themselves, and instruments that are made holy. The former focuses on what we need to do in order to cooperate with God's grace. We need to repent and make efforts to keep sin out of our lives. The other focuses on God's sovereign grace. It is He who ultimately makes us holy through the sanctifying work of the Holy Spirit (1 Peter 1:2; Romans 15:16; 2 Thessalonians 2:13).

The Lord prepares us to do His good work by purifying us and producing holiness in us. As a clean musical instrument is useful to the musician, so will a cleansed and holy disciple be a useful instrument in God's hands. No one can really do any effective work for the Lord without such holiness.

In a modern social climate where character and competencies are divorced (your personal life does not matter if you can get the job done), God's principle is all the more to be remembered. When a revival broke out in Samaria, a sorcerer apparently believed the gospel and was baptised, but God revealed his true condition. When he wanted special spiritual powers, Peter told him off by declaring that his heart was not right with God and that he was a captive to sin (Acts 8:18–23).

Timothy is to watch his personal holiness. He must remain a clean vessel. Leaders who are unclean vessels will deal with opponents through politics rather than ministry. They will be more concerned with self-preservation than in preserving the gospel. We must ensure that there is purity of life and doctrine within our hearts.

Why is it that the
church may have
both true and false
servants? Consider
the Lord's parable
of the wheat
and the tares
(Matthew 13:24–30).
What lessons can
we learn?

How do you
understand the
phrases "a man who
cleanses himself"
and "made holy"
(2 Timothy 2:21)?
Why is holiness
necessary to be
useful to the Master?
Consider your
usefulness to
the Lord.

Day 40

Read 2 Timothy 2:22–26

Timothy is to demonstrate two opposite actions ("flee" and "pursue", 2 Timothy 2:22) with the same seriousness and strength. He is to *flee* sin as if it is the plague. The "evil desires of youth" (v. 22) refer to those things that are opposed to the development of Christian maturity—sexual sins, impulsiveness, aggression, arrogance, unbridled ambition, and the like. It must be noted that older people can also suffer from the evil desires of youth, especially if they try to act like the young.

Secondly, Timothy is to *pursue* those things that are connected with mature Christian discipleship. In the words of theologian John Stott, he must "go in hot pursuit" of those virtues ("righteousness, faith, love and peace", v. 22) and habits that lead to godliness. He need not do this as a "lone ranger" Christian, but along with the Christian community who will encourage, support, and hold him accountable ("along with those who call on the Lord", v. 22).

The Christian life is not merely about avoiding sin, but also pursuing righteousness. The secret of holiness is in resolutely running away from sin and relentlessly running towards holiness. Without such holiness, it is impossible to please God or be useful to Him.

Paul then deals with how Timothy is to handle the opposition. He must avoid sin and be godly in his response. He must not enter into useless quarrels or step inside the boxing ring in response to the taunts of his opponents (v. 23). Instead, he should be "kind to everyone" (v. 24) and "gently instruct" (v. 25) his opponents. He is to be more like a patient and wise father than a quarrelsome, hot-blooded, and resentful sibling. By so doing, he will be living out his godliness and serving as a model of pastoral integrity and kindness.

In addition, he may win over his opponents. After all, the aim of ministry is not to win arguments, but to win people. He should counter their heresy by always harbouring the holy hope that they would repent (v. 25) and "come to their senses and escape from the trap of the devil" (v. 26). If so, they'll escape from the devil's grip and begin doing God's will instead of the devil's (v. 26). We should always have such noble hopes and prayers in our hearts even when encountering opposition.

ThinkThrough

Make a list of things you should flee from and another list of things you should pursue seriously. Is God saying anything specific about the direction, passion, and seriousness of your life?

Why is it more important to win people rather than arguments? How can this be practised in our relationships with "friends" and "enemies"? What should your inner hopes and prayers be when you minister and defend the truth?

Day 41

Read 2 Timothy 3:1–5

The "last days" in the Bible refer to the entire period from the ascension of Jesus to the cataclysmic end of history (Hebrews 1:2). Paul refers to this period here, focusing on how bad it will be in the future. These will be "terrible times" (2 Timothy 3:1) and full of terrible people. The people of the last days will show the cumulative effects of self-love and self-centredness.

Paul lists 19 characteristics of the terrible people of the last days. Most of them can be summarised in terms of misplaced love—love of self, money, and pleasure. God is love (1 John 4:8) and created us with a capacity to love. Hence the commands of Scripture are summarised as the call to love God wholeheartedly and to love our neighbours (Matthew 22:37–40). But fallen sinful human nature has perverted true love and turned it into love of self and things. The result: ugly human beings living in an ugly world.

Paul's list can be briefly examined as follows:

They love themselves above all (2 Timothy 3:2). This is the biggest problem. It produces all kinds of bad behaviour, from arrogance to slander. Human beings are obsessed with themselves, in what social critic Christopher Lasch called "the culture of narcissism". Martin Luther's observation about himself as he resisted the pope of his day is illuminating: "I am more afraid of my own heart than of the pope and all his cardinals. I have within me the great pope, Self." This is why the Christian life begins and is maintained by self-denial (Luke 9:23).

They love money (2 Timothy 3:2). The love of money is the source of many evils and has become a deadly obsession. The Bible calls greed idolatry (Colossians 3:5; Ephesians 5:5), showing that money is the god worshipped by many.

They love evil and that which is unholy instead of the good (2 Timothy 3:2–3), inverting values and calling good evil and evil good (Isaiah 5:20).

They love pleasure (2 Timothy 3:4). In pursuit of self-indulgent pleasure, they lose their self-control (v. 3).

Even the religious among them are guilty of a hollow religion (v. 5).

Paul's punch line is, "Have nothing to do with such people" (v. 5).

In essence, Christians must be different from the terrible people of the last days.

ThinkThrough

Why is self-love
the main human
problem? How
do we learn to
crucify the flesh
daily (Luke 9:23;
Galatians 2:20, 5:24)?
How does God's
grace enable us to
do this?

To what extent is
Paul's list real in
today's world? In
what way is there an
inversion of values
(Isaiah 5:20)?
How can Christians
keep themselves
from becoming
polluted by the
world (1 Corinthians
15:33)?

Day 42

Read 2 Timothy 3:6–9

The ungodliness of the world can easily creep into the church. All that is needed are ungodly false teachers and ungodly listeners.

Paul was aware that false teachers who shared the ungodliness of the last days were worming their way into homes and winning over "gullible women" (2 Timothy 3:6; see Genesis 3:1–7). The false teachers knew the weak spots and vulnerabilities of these women, who were "loaded down with sins and [were] swayed by all kinds of evil desires" (2 Timothy 3:6).

False teaching cashes in on sinful desires such as pride, greed, and lust, being attractive to those who love their sins more than their salvation; it also looks for knowledge without seeking to know God (Genesis 3:5–6). False teachers love perpetual students for the financial rewards they bring. They keep teaching their students, who do not learn anything of value. These students are "always learning but never able to come to a knowledge of the truth" (2 Timothy 3:7). Such false worldly knowledge may promise to teach us about *something* but can never introduce us to the *Someone* (Jesus) we must know in order to be saved.

To ignorant and deceived people, false teachers may appear attractive and persuasive. Such was the case with the Egyptian magicians Jannes and Jambres, who were able to reproduce Moses' miracle of turning a staff into a snake (Exodus 7:8–12). Such superficial success can lull people into deception. But when Aaron's staff swallowed up those of the magicians', the deception was clearly exposed. All deceptions will eventually be exposed. Therefore, Paul is confident that the folly of the false teachers (and their students) "will be clear to everyone" (2 Timothy 3:9). Their "depraved minds" (3:8) will be evident.

Today, false teachers and deceptive teachings can easily enter homes through the Internet and other mass media. The challenges for the church are enormous. **Never has there been a greater need for the faithful teaching of God's Word than in our modern day.** It is so easy for Christians who are exposed to the many influences of the world, to fall into serious errors in belief and lifestyle. With the erosion of the authority of the pulpit and the profusion of false teachings, there is much need for fervent praying and faithful preaching.

Why is false teaching attractive to many people? What does it say about them and the false teachers? How can we know if a teaching is false?

In what ways is Satan worming his way into people's hearts and homes today? What can the church do to counter this? What confidence can we have amid this struggle?

Day 43

Read 2 Timothy 3:10–13

It is imperative for Christians to be different from the godless people of the last days. For Timothy, his teaching is also to be different from that of the false teachers. Paul offers his own life as a model. There is no better teacher than one who walks his talk.

Paul reminds Timothy of his teaching, with which Timothy was very familiar (2 Timothy 3:10). Paul took his teaching ministry seriously, never seeking to please men or even himself, but only God who had called him (1 Corinthians 4:1–4; Galatians 1:9–10; 1 Thessalonians 2:2–6). His teaching was always focused on Christ and His gospel (1 Corinthians 2:2) and, unlike the false teachers, he did not peddle it for profit (2 Corinthians 2:17).

Paul taught devotion to Christ and obedience to Him. He demonstrated his sermons with his life. He reminds Timothy of his "way of life", which was characterised by the godliness found in his "purpose, faith, patience, love, endurance, persecutions, sufferings" (2 Timothy 3:10–11). Paul's central purposes of bringing glory to God and the gospel to the Gentiles were shown in his deep trust in God, his patience with difficult people, his endurance in difficult circumstances, and his acceptance of suffering as a part of his calling (Acts 9:16). These were all indications of his exemplary and inspiring godliness. Such should be the character of Christians living in a godless world.

Godly Christians should not be surprised if they are persecuted by the world in the last days (2 Timothy 3:12). This comment from a faithful apostle awaiting a death sentence brings comfort to Christians undergoing persecution. Paul is realistic in his expectation that "evildoers and impostors will go from bad to worse" (3:13). They will continue to deceive and be deceived (3:13), but the Christian must not lose heart.

As we live in the darkening world of the last days, and as godlessness increases, we must avoid two things. Firstly, we must not join the world. We must remember Scottish theologian P. T. Forsyth's wise words: "Unless there is within us that which is above us, we shall soon yield to that which is about us." Secondly, as we suffer persecution in the hands of an unbelieving and disobedient world, we must continue to show godliness and shine like stars in the night sky (Philippians 2:15).

Read Acts 13:50; 14:5,19–20 to understand Paul's reference (2 Timothy 3:11) to his first missionary journey, where he suffered much persecution in various cities. Paul went back to these cities on his way back to Antioch (Acts 14:21–22). What does this say about Paul's response to persecution and his faith in God (2 Timothy 3:10–11)?

How can Christians living in a "crooked and depraved generation" (Philippians 2:15) shine like stars instead of being snuffed out or losing their shine? How are you shining?

Day 44

Read 2 Timothy 3:14–17

Paul refers to two resources that would help Timothy maintain his Christian character in the godless world of the last days: godly mentors and Scripture.

Instead of giving in to the godless ways of the world or giving up godliness, Timothy is urged by Paul to "continue in what you have learned and have become convinced of" (2 Timothy 3:14). This is possible because "you know those from whom you learned it" (v. 14), which refers to Paul as well as Timothy's mother and grandmother. They were key mentors in Timothy's life and spiritual formation.

We see here the power of godly mentoring in helping Christians to stand firm amid a worsening world. Our mentors are like the "great cloud of witnesses" who cheer us on the way so that we can run the race faithfully and finish it successfully (Hebrews 12:1). Remembering our mentors and what they have taught us will help us to walk uprightly in a sinful world.

The second great resource is Scripture. Paul reminds Timothy that from a young age he had learned the Scriptures (thanks to the faithful mentors in his family) and had been shaped by them (2 Timothy 3:15). He must continue to hold on to God's Word and live by it.

Scripture makes us wise and leads us to salvation in Christ (v. 15). We will read the Bible seriously when we remember its origins and purpose (v. 16). It is the God-breathed, inspired revelation of God, which has power to teach, rebuke, correct, and train us in righteousness.

In other words, it is necessary that we read the Bible carefully with a view to letting it shape, confront, and guide us if we are to grow in Christ. John Stott is right in observing that "Scripture is the chief means which God employs to bring the 'man of God' to maturity". Not only does the Bible help to produce *Christian character* (as the Holy Spirit brings God's Word into our lives), but it also helps to produce *Christian ministry* as the believer is "thoroughly equipped for every good work" (v. 17). In the sinful world of the last days, both Christian character and ministry are greatly needed.

Who are your
mentors? How are
you helped to be
faithful to God by
their example and
teaching? Are you
such a mentor to
others?

How has the Bible
taught, rebuked,
corrected, and
trained you in recent
days? How can
you improve your
Bible reading and
meditation so that
Christian character
and ministry can
be more powerfully
expressed in
your life?

Day 45

Read 2 Timothy 4:1–5

n the terrible world of the last days, Christian character must be demonstrated and Christian ministry must continue effectively. There is no place for withdrawal from the world. For Timothy, his main ministry as a pastor was teaching—especially amid popular but dangerous false teachings. In his closing words, Paul issues another charge to Timothy: "Preach the Word" (2 Timothy 4:1–2).

The *motive* for this ministry is drawn from two factors: the authority of God, and the urgency of the hour. Christians must be faithful and diligent in their ministry because God has commanded it. Paul issues the charge in the presence of God and His Son (v. 1)—a very serious and solemn affair. When facing severe opposition, Timothy would be heartened to know that he was doing God's bidding in God's presence. It is an urgent ministry because Christ is going to appear soon (v. 1). The end is near and the eternal destiny of people is at stake. As biblical scholar Adam Clarke puts it, "The Judge is at the door, and to every man eternity is at hand!" Timothy must preach "in season and out of season" (v. 2)—at every opportunity.

The central *message* of this ministry is the Word of God (v. 2). Unlike the false teachers who were experts in enticing myths (v. 4), the people of God must stick to the Word and teach it faithfully, for it is the Word that leads people to Christ and His salvation. Even if the crowds had no appetite for sound doctrine (vv. 3–4), the faithful pastor must keep his head, be willing to suffer, and do all that is needed (v. 5).

The *modes* of ministry include correcting, rebuking, and encouraging (v. 2). Those who are doubting must be convinced, those in the wrong must be converted, and those who are suffering must be comforted. The faithful preaching of the Word will produce such effects in the hearers. The end result is salvation and Christian maturity.

The manner of ministry is Christ-likeness (v. 2). The godly teacher must teach with Christ-like character ("great patience") and diligence ("careful instruction"). Such ministry will produce lasting fruits and bring glory to God.

Paul indicates that in the last days, people will have a "Do-It-Yourself" attitude to religion. They will choose teachers to "suit their own desires" and who will teach "what their itching ears want to hear" (2 Timothy 4:3). To what extent do you see this today? Why is this so?

Do you believe in the urgency of the hour? What implications are there for all your relationships and how you live?

Day 46

Read 2 Timothy 4:6–7

At the end of his letter, Paul deals with some personal matters. He opens his heart to reveal how he feels about his approaching martyrdom, his personal needs, and his unshakeable faith in God.

Paul observes that "the time for [his] departure is near" (2 Timothy 4:6). The Greek expression refers to the unmooring of a ship. Paul's busy and eventful earthly journey was about to end. He was not going to die in a cosy bed surrounded by gentle people and music. Instead, Paul was beheaded as a criminal. His death was a "drink offering" (4:6). Despite the painful, violent, and humiliating circumstances, the resilient apostle could rejoice that he was privileged to be sharing "in [Christ's] sufferings, becoming like him in his death" (Philippians 3:10).

It was time to review his life for one last time. Paul was thankful to the Lord for His grace and power. He declares three great statements with much joy and satisfaction (2 Timothy 4:7). The three statements resemble the three metaphors he used in 2 Timothy 2:3–6.

"I have fought the good fight". The Greek word for "fight" is related to the word "agony". Paul knew that the Christian life is a bruising battle against the devil, flesh, and world. He did not spare any effort in fighting. The good fight involves faithfully and firmly standing our ground. It is fought not with the weapons of the world (human strategy and might, wealth, and power), but with the armour and sword of God (2 Corinthians 10:3–4; Ephesians 6:10–18). After many years of ministry, Paul was still standing in battle as Christ's loyal and valiant soldier, bearing the "marks of Jesus" on his body (Galatians 6:17).

"I have finished the race". Some people start well but fail to finish the race. Paul ran every lap and was now running the home stretch. It must have been an exhilarating feeling. He had always wanted to "finish the race and complete the task" (Acts 20:24).

"I have kept the faith". Paul had not dropped the baton (the gospel), but successfully passed it on to successors like Timothy and Titus. It must have been with a sense of elation that he realised that while his life was ending, the gospel mission would continue to grow from strength to strength. The messenger may die, but the message lives on.

Review your life in terms of the fight, the race, and the faith. How would you describe each of them? What challenges are you facing? How is God helping you?

How would you urge others to "finish the race and complete the task" (Acts 20:24)? How can pain and suffering detract someone from pursuing this noble goal?

Day 47

Read 2 Timothy 4:8

Having reviewed his past with gratitude, Paul now looks forward to the future with much anticipation. He knew that his Lord would award to him "the crown of righteousness" (2 Timothy 4:8). Here, Paul continues his metaphor of the Christian life as a race. The winners in the Greek Games would be honoured with crowns made of olive or laurel leaves. It was a great achievement to be able to wear this victor's crown. When the champions returned home, they would be welcomed with great fanfare.

The crown that Paul would be given would be a different kind. Firstly, it "will never fade way", but will "last for ever" (1 Peter 5:4; 1 Corinthians 9:25). The crown won at the Games would eventually wither—this is the fate of all earthly crowns. But the crowns in heaven are eternal.

Secondly, the heavenly crown would be awarded by the "righteous Judge" himself. His judgment is perfect and final, full of wisdom and justice. All earthly crown-givers would pale in comparison to the One who gives the heavenly crown.

Thirdly, the heavenly crown would be worn with great humility. It cannot sit comfortably on proud and self-congratulatory heads. In a heavenly scene that the apostle John witnessed, the 24 elders seated on thrones would fall down before Jesus. "They lay their crowns before the throne" (Revelation 4:10). The crown would not be a sign of personal achievement, but of God's mercy and grace.

Fourthly, the crown would be given to "all who have longed for his appearing" (2 Timothy 4:8). It would not be for the elite only, but for everyone who believed in Jesus and obeyed Him, waiting for His return. In other words, while everyone in heaven will have a crown, there will be no hidden competition over who has the best crown. The attention will not be on the crown wearers, but on the glorious crown Giver.

Those who mistakenly see the heavenly crown as a trophy given for religious performance will be sorely disappointed. It is not something earned, but something given graciously by the God who "sees what is done in secret" (Matthew 6:4).

The reward will not be earthly honours and possessions, but the uninterrupted presence of Jesus and the joy of seeing His face (Psalm 27:4).

What does the Bible teach about rewards in heaven? How can such teaching be misunderstood? How do you think you will be rewarded in heaven?

Which of the four points about the heavenly crown speaks to you most powerfully? Why? Read the parable of the vineyard workers in Matthew 20:1–16. What does it say about God's rewards?

Day 48

Read 2 Timothy 4:9–13

As a prisoner waiting to be sentenced to death, Paul reveals his various needs. In so doing, he reveals a godly and balanced perspective of human life.

Firstly, Paul refers to the cloak that he had left with Carpus in Troas (probably when he was arrested; 2 Timothy 4:13). With winter approaching when the nights could be bitterly cold, Paul requests that Timothy bring the cloak to keep him warm. As retired Presbyterian minister Gary Demarest reflects, "How comforting to know that this spiritual giant didn't find any virtue in needless shivering!" The body must not be abused through extreme ascetic practices (self-denial) or indulged through sinful lifestyles. The "harsh treatment of the body" will produce ill-health rather than holiness, and is not a biblical prescription (Colossians 2:23).

The body must also not be allowed to become a slave to sin (Romans 6:12–13). Jesus taught that it is "better for you to lose one part of your body than for your whole body to go into hell" (Matthew 5:30). The body is the temple of the Holy Spirit (1 Corinthians 6:19) and must be consecrated as a living sacrifice in submission and service to the Lord (Romans 12:1).

Secondly, Paul refers to his scrolls and parchments (2 Timothy 4:13). These were probably books, writing material, and the Scriptures. Even in his final days, Paul wanted to meet his intellectual needs. There are two extremes to be avoided: anti-intellectualism and sterile intellectualism. Paul had a healthy and good mind that he used for God's service. He read widely and deeply. Such reading brings useful knowledge, healing, and transformation.

Thirdly, Paul reveals his social needs. He needed friends in this crisis. Some, like Demas, had deserted him, while others were away on mission (2 Timothy 4:10). Only his old and trusted friend Luke was with him (v. 11). Paul wanted very much to see Timothy (v. 9) and Mark (v. 11). He had problems with Mark in the past (Acts 15:36–41), but was now reconciled with him. During his ministry, Paul had developed many deep friendships (see Romans 16, Colossians 4:7–18). Before his death, he longed to see some younger friends, perhaps to see that the gospel would continue to be preached faithfully and for mutual encouragement.

The most important need is dealt with in the next section.

Why are both extreme asceticism and the indulgence of the body unhelpful? How should Christians handle their bodies in a world saturated with physical pampering and addictions?

Review the various needs you have. How would you differentiate between legitimate needs and sinful wants? Are there needs you tend to neglect because of busyness, laziness, or distraction?

Day 49

Read 2 Timothy 4:14–18

Paul was in prison probably because of Alexander the metalworker (2 Timothy 4:14–15). It is possible that Alexander was once serving with Paul, but now had become an apostate and an enemy of Paul. He could have been a spy for the state who betrayed Paul. This betrayal must have hurt Paul in many ways.

Paul had an initial trial at which he felt abandoned by friends. The words "no one" and "everyone" (4:16) express his sadness and pain. But he was not angry or resentful. Like Jesus who prayed on the cross for his tormentors (Luke 23:34), Paul prayed for his friends who had fled when he needed them most (2 Timothy 4:16).

Though abandoned by earthly friends, Paul had a heavenly Friend who stood at his side and strengthened him (4:17). Paul states some wonderful truths about Jesus, deeply experienced at this final stage of his life.

The Presence of Christ. "The Lord stood at my side" (4:17). God has promised to be with His people (Exodus 3:12; Joshua 1:5; Matthew 28:20), and Paul had already written that there is nothing anywhere that can separate us from God's love (Romans 8:38–39). He testified that the Lord had helped him all the way (Acts 26:22). Christ, our Immanuel ("God with us"), is always present with His servants, even in the darkest prison.

The Purpose of Christ. Though Paul may have had many questions regarding his imprisonment, he knew that there was divine purpose. He considered himself to be Christ's (not Caesar's) prisoner (2 Timothy 1:8). At his first trial, as Paul defended his message and actions, he had the unique opportunity to share the gospel with some of the most powerful people in Rome (Acts 9:15; 25:25). Even in his painful isolation, Paul could rejoice that through him the gospel was "fully proclaimed" (2 Timothy 4:17). He was still useful to his Lord in a uniquely strategic way.

The Promise of Christ. Reflecting on his first trial, Paul testifies that the Lord delivered him "from the lion's mouth" (4:17; see Daniel 6:15–23). He was confident that the Lord would rescue him "from every evil attack" and bring him "safely to his heavenly kingdom" (2 Timothy 4:18). **Paul may be martyred, but he knew that he was safe in his Lord's hands** (John 10:28). The Lord would keep His promise (Matthew 10:28–32).

Have you experienced the Lord standing near you (2 Timothy 4:17; Acts 23:11)? What comfort did it bring you? Why is it important to develop an awareness of the Lord's presence in our lives? How can you do it?

Paul was an evangelist even as a prisoner. What does it say about his loyalty to Christ and his passion for the gospel? How does trusting Christ's promises help us to do His work in all situations?

Day 50

Read 2 Timothy 4:19–22

We come to the last written words of the apostle Paul. There is no fanfare, only the simple expression of his love for the Lord and His people. It is all the more moving for its sincerity and depth.

In Paul's extensive travels and widespread ministry, he had met and worked with numerous people and had come to love them deeply. It was customary to end letters with some form of greetings and a benediction. Here, Paul not only sent general greetings, but also named specific individuals. This demonstrates that Paul's love for his fellow believers was not just some general sentiment that did not mean much—he truly loved and prayed for specific people.

Paul ended his epistle to the Romans by naming more than 19 people. Here, in three short verses, he mentions 10 individuals and "all the brothers and sisters". Priscilla and Aquila were Paul's close friends and co-workers, whom he had first met in Corinth (Acts 18:1–2). They served the Lord faithfully and were also mentioned in the final greetings in Romans 16 and 1 Corinthians 16. Onesiphorus (2 Timothy 1:16–18) had been greatly helpful to Paul during his imprisonment. Paul sends greetings to his family with much appreciation and love. Erastus, Corinth's director of public works (Romans 16:23), became an assistant to Paul and was well known to Timothy (Acts 19:22).

Trophimus, from Ephesus, was another of Paul's associates (Acts 20:4; 21:29). It must have been difficult for Paul to leave him sick in Miletus; no doubt Paul prayed often for his healing. The others mentioned were Roman believers who, together with Luke, must have provided comfort and help to Paul. Paul urges Timothy to come to him quickly (2 Timothy 4:21); such was his longing to see him one last time.

Finally, Paul ends with a benediction that the Lord would be with Timothy's spirit and that His grace would be evident in his life (4:22). The Lord's presence and His providential grace and power would help Timothy to be like Paul—faithful to the end.

And so concludes this great apostle, who left behind many churches he had founded, many friends and Christian communities, and a body of literature that forms half of the New Testament books. Paul's life and ministry were remarkable because he trusted, loved, and served his remarkable Lord.

Some writers portray Paul as a task-driven missionary. What does this passage reveal about the real Paul? What evidence can you find to show that Paul cared for people and that he took relationships seriously? What implications are there for you?

What do you think is Paul's greatest legacy? What did he leave behind? What legacy do you think you will leave behind when your earthly journey is over? What are you doing about it today?

Going Deeper in Your Walk with Christ

In the letters of the New Testament, we have the explanation of Jesus Christ and the Christian way of living. Journey through the letters written by apostle Paul to discover and explore the deep truths and the deep experience of knowing and following Jesus Christ.

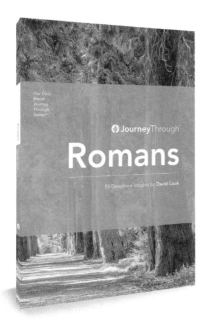

Journey Through

Romans

The book of Romans outlines what Christians believe and explains God's perfect plan in bringing sinners back to Him. More than any other book in the Bible, it has played a crucial role in shaping church history, and has been called the greatest theological document ever written. Many have found Romans a daunting book to study. But David Cook writes in a style that makes difficult truths easy to understand. Rediscover why the gospel is such good news, and walk away with a deeper appreciation of what and why you believe.

David Cook was Principal of the Sydney Missionary and Bible College for 26 years. He is an accomplished writer and has authored Bible commentaries, books on the Minor Prophets, and several Bible study guides.

Journey Through

Colossians & Philemon

If the Christian life is like a race, how do we ensure that we finish the race, and finish strong? Let the letters to the Colossians and Philemon serve as a guide and source of encouragement as you press on towards this goal. In his letter to the Colossians, the apostle Paul urges the young church to grow strong in Christ and reminds them of His promises, character, and authority. In the letter to Philemon, Paul gives us a wonderful insight into the dynamic, transforming nature of Christian fellowship. Dig into these letters and let the teachings within guide you towards maturity in Christ Jesus.

Mike Raiter is a preacher, preaching trainer, and a former Principal of the Melbourne School of Theology in Australia. He is now the Director of Centre for Biblical Preaching and the author of a number of books, including *Stirrings of the Soul*, which won the 2004 Australian Christian Book of the year award.

Want to catch up on any back copies you may have missed from *Journey Through*? The series so far is available for purchase at

discoveryhouse.org.uk

For information on our resources, visit **ourdailybread.org**. Alternatively, please contact the office nearest you from the list below, or go to **ourdailybread.org/locations** for the complete list of offices.

BELARUS
Our Daily Bread Ministries
PO Box 82, Minsk, Belarus 220107
belarus@odb.org • (375-17) 2854657; (375-29) 9168799

GERMANY
Our Daily Bread Ministries e.V.
Schulstraße 42, 79540 Lörrach
deutsch@odb.org

IRELAND
Our Daily Bread Ministries
64 Baggot Street Lower, Dublin 2, D02 XC62
ireland@odb.org • +353 (0) 1676 7315

RUSSIA
MISSION Our Daily Bread
PO Box "Our Daily Bread",
str.Vokzalnaya 2, Smolensk, Russia 214961
russia@odb.org • 8(4812)660849; +7(951)7028049

UKRAINE
Christian Mission Our Daily Bread
PO Box 533, Kiev, Ukraine 01004
ukraine@odb.org • +380964407374; +380632112446

UNITED KINGDOM (Europe Regional Office)
Our Daily Bread Ministries
PO Box 1, Millhead, Carnforth, LA5 9ES
europe@odb.org • +44 (0)15395 64149

ourdailybread.org

Sign up to *Journey Through*

We would love to support you with the *Journey Through* series! Please be aware we can only provide one copy of each future *Journey Through* book per reader (previous books from the series are available to purchase).

If you know of other people who would be interested in this series, we can send you introductory *Journey Through* booklets to pass onto them (which include details on how they can easily sign up for the books themselves).

☐ **I would like to regularly receive the *Journey Through* series**

☐ **Please send me ___ copies of the *Journey Through* introductory booklet**

Just complete and return this sign up form to us at:

Our Daily Bread Ministries, PO Box 1, Millhead, Carnforth, LA5 9ES, United Kingdom

Here at Our Daily Bread Ministries we take your privacy seriously. We will only use this personal information to manage your account, and regularly provide you with *Journey Through* series books and offers of other resources, three ministry update letters each year, and occasional additional mailings with news that's relevant to you. We will also send you ministry updates and details of Discovery House products by email if you agree to this. In order to do this we share your details with our UK-based mailing house and Our Daily Bread Ministries in the US. We do not sell or share personal information with anyone for marketing purposes.

Please do not complete and sign this form for anyone but yourself. You do not need to complete this form if you already receive regular copies of *Journey Through* from us.

Full Name (Mr/Mrs/Miss/Ms): _____

Address: _____

_____

Postcode: _____ Tel: _____

Email: _____

☐ I would like to receive email updates and details of Discovery House products.

Signature: _____

All our resources, including *Journey Through*, are available without cost. Many people, making even the smallest of donations, enable Our Daily Bread Ministries to reach others with the life-changing wisdom of the Bible. We are not funded or endowed by any group or denomination.